The Ardis Anthology of New American Poetry

edited by
DAVID RIGSBEE
ELLENDEA PROFFER

Ardis / Ann Arbor

ACKNOWLEDGEMENTS

ALEXANDER, CHARLOTTE: "The Write-Off" printed by permission of the
author. ALEXANDER, PAMELA: "interface," "Flight," and "Air" printed by
permission of the author. ALTHAUS, KEITH: "Traveling in Europe" (first
published in *Poetry*), copyright 1974 by the Modern Poetry Association, re-
printed by permission of Daryl Hine; "Indian Summer Garden Party" (first
published in *Harper's*) and "The Somnambulist Blue" (first published in *The
Greensboro Review*), reprinted by permission of the author; "Poem," "In the
Hammersmith Public Library" and "Middle River" printed by permission of
the author. AXELROD, MARK: all works printed by permission of the author.
BALDWIN, NEIL: "Gaining, with departure," printed by permission of the
author. BAYES, RON: "The Casketmaker" and "The Philadelphia Airport,"
from *The Casketmaker*, copyright Ron H. Bayes, reprinted by permission of
the author. BENNETT, BRUCE: "The True Story of Snow White" (first pub-
lished in *Mosaic*), reprinted by permission of the author. BERRY, D.C.:
"Epistle to Celia" (first published in *Gone Soft*) and "To the Woodville Depot"
(first published in *New South Writing*), reprinted by permission of the author.
BERRYHILL, MICHAEL: "For Borges" (first published in *The American Re-
view/New American Review*), reprinted by permission of the author. "Rheto-
ric," printed by permission of the author. BROWN, HUNTER: "Rivage,"
printed by permission of the author. BURKARD, MICHAEL: "The Victim" and
"Wren: Three Mirrors" (both 1st pub'd. in *Poetry*),©MPA, reprinted by permis-
sion of the publisher; "Gaslight" and "(Untitled)," printed by permission of
the author. CANTRELL, CHARLES: "The Amputee" (first published in *Ab-
raxas*), reprinted by permission of the publisher; "Aladdin's Lamp," printed
by permission of the author. CHAMBERLAIN, MARISHA: "No Respect for
Authority," printed by permission of the author. CHILDERS, DAVID: "Hunt"
(first published in *Carolina Quarterly*), reprinted by permission of the author;
"South Carolina Baptismal Procession," printed by permission of the author.
COLLINS, BILLY: "Shock" (first published in *The Midatlantic Review*), re-
printed by permission of the author; "Library," "Bad Dreams" and "Sentence,"
printed by permission of the author. DACEY, PHILIP: "Chain Letter" and
"Form Rejection Letter" (both first published in *Shenandoah*), copyright
1972 and 1973 (respectively) by *Shenandoah*, reprinted by permission of the
publisher; "Mystery Baseball" (first published in *Prairie Schooner*), copyright
1972 by the University of Nebraska Press, reprinted by permission of the pub-
lisher; "The Rowboat" (first published in *Poetry*), copyright 1974 by the
Modern Poetry Association, reprinted by permission of Daryl Hine; "The Rise
and Fall" (first published in *Nimrod*), reprinted by permission of the publisher;
"Anniversary" (first published in *Sou'wester*), reprinted by permission of the
author. DEAGON, ANN: "The Death of Phidias" (first published in *Carolina
Quarterly*), reprinted by permission of the publisher; "The Owl Pellet" (first
published in *Carbon 14*, U. of Mass. Press, 1974), reprinted by permission of
the publisher; "Jigsaw Puzzle" (first published in *Aura*), reprinted by permis-
sion of the publisher; "Going Under" (first published in *Crucible*), reprinted

by permission of the publisher. FLAHERTY, DOUG: "For a Girl Whose Slow Dying Called for My Blood" (first published in *To Keep the Blood from Drowning*, Second Coming Press, 1976), reprinted by permission of the publisher. FRANK, PETER: "On the Death of My Beard," printed by permission of the author. FROST, CAROL: "The Salt Lesson" (first published in *The Salt Lesson*, Graywolf Press, 1976), reprinted by permission of the publisher; "Night Is No More Or Less Important Than Bad Circles Or 'Ksing'," printed by permission of the author. GALLAGHER, TESS: "The Woman Who Raised Goats," "A Poem in Translation," "Rhododendrons" and "Time Lapse With Tulips," printed by permission of the author. GEORGE, EMERY: "Grief," "Projects" and "Weatherman of Sorrows," printed by permission of the author. GIBSON, MARGARET: "Lunes" (first published in *Lillabulero*), "Apples" (first published in *The Seneca Review*), "A Grammar of the Soul" (first published in *Shenandoah*) and "Octobering" (first published in *The Painted Bride Quarterly*), reprinted by permission of the author. GIOSEFFI, DANIELA: "Some Slippery Afternoon" (first published in *Choice*) and "Eggs" (published in *Ms.* and *Modern Poetry Studies*), reprinted by permission of the author; "Through the Eye of the Needle," printed by permission of the author. GOEDICKE, PATRICIA: "At Every Major Airport" (first published in *Epoch*), reprinted by permission of the publisher; "Success Story" (first published in *Crazy Horse*), reprinted by permission of the author; "Escalator," from *For the Four Corners*, Ithaca House, reprinted by permission of the publisher; "After the Second Operation" (first published in *New Letters*), reprinted by permission of the publisher; "Where We Are Going" and "The Dog Who Came From Nowhere," printed by permission of the author. GOODMAN, RYAH TUMARKIN: "Silence Spoke With Your Voice" (first published in *The Atlantic*) and "Ancestors" (first published in *The Chicago Tribune*), reprinted by permission of the author; "Portrait" and "The Business of Living," printed by permission of the author. GREGG, LINDA: "Figures Near a Bridge," For My Friend Michele (1966-1972)," "The Men Like Salmon," "The Apparent," "Andromache Afterwards" and "Not Singing," printed by permission of the author. HADAS, RACHEL: "Trial," printed by permission of the author. HAHN, ROBERT: "Words From the Housewife," "To the Stolen Children," "Interrogation," "Getting Through the Fifties: The Starkweather Case Revisited" and "A Bad Dream in the Commune," all from *Crimes*, Lynx House Press, 1976, reprinted by permission of the author. HARRIS, MARIE: "Interstate" (portions of which have appeared in *Truck, Aspect, 13th Moon, Clown War* and *Raw Honey* (AliceJamesBooks)), reprinted by permission of the author. HARTMAN, CHARLES O.: "Mastodon" (first published in *Poetry Northwest*), reprinted by permission of the author; "A Prayer for Violets" (first published in *Descant*), reprinted by permission of the author; "To Shadow" (first published in *Poetry*), copyright 1974 by the Modern Poetry Association, reprinted by permission of the publisher; "Before My Father" and "Milkweed" (both first published in *Poetry*), both copyright 1975 by the Modern Poetry Association, reprinted by permission of the publisher. HARTMAN, SUSAN: "In the Generation that Laughed at Me" and "After His Death" (both first published in *Hanging Loose*), reprinted by permission of the author. HEATH, WILLIAM: "Haystack Calhoun"(first published in *The Transylvanian*), reprinted by permission of the author. HIGGINSON, WILLIAM J.: "The Loves and Lays of William J. Higginson" and "On Reading Lao-Tzu," both from *A 30-Minute Reading, Xtras No. 7*, copyright 1976 by William J. Higginson, reprinted by permission of the publisher. HOGAN, MICHAEL: "Letter From My Son" and "A Quiet Orderly Life," both from *Letters For My Son*, Unicorn Press, 1975, copyright Michael Hogan, reprinted by permission of the author. HOUSE, TOM: "Parable of the Sidewalk Tellers" (first published in *Nausea*), reprinted by permission of the author. JAHNS, T.R.: "Utility," printed by permission of the author. JOHNSON, LEMUEL: selections from *Hand on the Navel* printed by permission of the author. JOHNSON, LORING: "Untitled" (first published in *Changes*), reprinted by permission of the publisher. KAMENETZ, RODGER: "Biograph" (first published in *Carolina Quarterly*), reprinted by permission of the author; "Christopher Magisto" (first published in *pendulum 1973: the johns hopkins university*), reprinted by permission of the publisher. KATZ, JANE: "Dressing for Our Spring Party," "Photograph of the Hanging Pianos" and "The Fields of the Country," printed

(first published in *Shenandoah*), "Claiming Kin" (first published in *The Iowa Review*) and "Farm Wife" (first published in *The Iowa Review*), all reprinted by permission of the author. WALLACE, RONALD: "One Hook" (first published in an alternate version in *The Iowa Review*), reprinted by permission of the author. WARDELL, W.S.: "2," "6" and "27," all printed by permission of the author. WATERS, MICHAEL: "Leaves & Ashes," "Wedding Poem," "Leaving America," "The Dead" and "Night Fishing," all from *Fish Light*, Ithaca House, 1975, reprinted by permission from the publisher. WIEDER, LAURANCE: "A Letter to His Sister," from *No Harm Done*, copyright 1975 by Ardis, reprinted by permission of the publisher; "The Paradise Rug," printed by permission of the author. WILLIAMS, RICHARD: "Savarin," "Rita Rio," "The Fable of the Airplanes" and "The Way It Is," printed by permission of the author. YVONNE: "She-Who-Opens" and "1946," printed by permission of the author. ZIEGLER, ALAN: "Displacement," "Waiting for the Bus," "Sunday Night," "Curtain Call" and "The Guest," printed by permission of the author. ZIRLIN, LARRY: "When Greenberg Speaks, Can a Poem Be Far Behind?" and "Dream Girl," printed by permission of the author. ZU-BOLTON, AHMOS: "Blackjack Moses (first published in *Pure Light Journal*), "the governor of ollie street" (first published in *Obsidian*) and "thru Blue eyes" (first published in *Hoo-Doo BlackSeries*), all copyright Ahmos Zu-Bolton, reprinted by permission of the author.

EDITORS' NOTE

This is an anthology of poems, not poets. It demonstrates something of the diversity of American poetry today. The concerns in the poems range from the history of one man's neurosis (in the form of a recipe) to meditations on the terrors of mystery baseball. The poems speak of urban violence, war, the solace of nature, the fractures of the family, the joys and pains of sex and love. While many of these themes are the eternal stuff of poetry, the specifics of the poems mark them our time and place: bar girls lament in Vietnam; a man with a gun enters a White Castle restaurant; the Interstate highway becomes a metaphor; Jungian archetypes illuminate the new war between the sexes.

In making the selections we tried to concentrate on poets who had not published more than one book, though in some instances, and for various reasons, we made exceptions. The process of selection itself continued for almost two years as public announcements brought hundreds of submissions to Ardis. The fact that the editors' tastes and sensibilities are quite different helped to avoid homogeneous content. But apart from this, we tried to remain free of strong editorial bias and to let the poems attempt to make their own space. In doing so, the idea of the anthology evolved from one spotlighting poets to one simply of poems. As a consequence it is natural that the size of one poet's selection might differ from another's. In addition, we included, thanks to a suggestion by David Ignatow, a number of works by poets who have not had extensive publication in book form and who do not fall under the attractive rubric, "younger poet." (Though there are extremes on either side, most of the poets are between twenty-five and thirty-five.) Finally, we have included a few long poems, because while they rarely find their way into anthologies, they too are representative of one of American poetry's preoccupations.

David Rigsbee
Ellendea Proffer

CONTENTS

ALPHABETICAL LIST OF CONTRIBUTORS

THE ARDIS ANTHOLOGY OF NEW AMERICAN POETRY

RICHARD WILLIAMS

Savarin

I

Take one chicken from three to five pounds,
coming home from an evening on the town,
salt it with garlic and pepper,
then melt one-half stick of butter
that signals the end of it
in a pan with one spoon of tarragon,
all that there was,
our civilization,
and three-fourths cup white wine.

Stuff the chicken with the green ends
of spring onions, pour on simmering mixture
hot in the memory
from the pan, then cook
what seethes on the brain
in a moderate oven for forty-five
passing in sequence
minutes plus ten for each pound if cold
like time on end, like scallops
and seven if at room temperature. Serve

with risotto and haricots verts
on the beach
à maître d'hôtel. White wine.

II

Marinate two veal chops, rather thick,
where is my youth,
with the juice of two lemons, garlic salt,
where did it go,
and one teaspoon of crushed thyme. While
the Lord

in the marinade, saute one bell pepper
speaks of His passion
and one onion, diced, in one-half stick of butter
as if it were a nail just bolted
until tender. Remove the vegetables
to my neighbor's eyes
and cook the chops on top of the stove
I hate them
in the butter residue for fifteen minutes,
let them go blind
turning them once in the meantime,
those fools.

Add the vegetables along with one can of
hate, but with
tomatoes to pilaf, and serve with a rosé
piety.

III

Where are the snows of yesteryear,
in one-half stick of butter sauté three crushed*
goons who have besieged me
one-half teaspoon of oregano, and one teaspoon
        of parsley
with their angry looks.

After ten minutes of slow simmering, add
an eight-ounce can of minced clams;
allow this to simmer for five to ten minutes

or is He?
and serve over spinach noodles.

White wine and perhaps a salad of bell pepper
I've often wondered
and tomato; tarragon dressing.

*(garlic cloves, one tablespoon of sweet basil)

IV
Especially coming home late when I
lather a three to four pound rump roast
with garlic salt, pepper, and marjoram,
sear it for a few minutes on top of the stove
speak of love
with high heat, being careful to brown all
sides. Surround with three sliced onions
their beautiful backs
in butter
and one-third cup of water,

then cook for twenty-five minutes per pound at 325
times I've seen Satan, too,
under a tent of aluminum, and serve hot with
devils by his side, eating
baked potatoes, sour cream, a tossed salad,
pigs-feet,
and a hearty burgundy.

V
For each one-half pound of steak, cook one-half
the pain
a bell pepper, one-half of an onion
makes for a winsome frolic through bus terminals
in two or three tablespoons of butter slowly
late at night
until tender. Slice the steak into thin strips
when only the masks are out
and marinate with enough Worcestershire
to make me quiver, and
to coat each piece evenly and sparingly
dream of them.

O Jesus!
Salt and pepper the vegetables and the steak.
I've been cold too long.
Remove vegetables from the pan and cook
past my prime

the steak in the butter for a few minutes,
I've written books on religion
then add the vegetables, stir a few minutes
to see visions
until just done, still slightly rare, and serve
topped with a quartered tomato
over rice. Red wine.

VI
For dessert spread a mixture of melted butter
over the hands
and honey over toast; serve with coffee and tea
then look at them
and light up a cigarette, or a cigar
or their host.

Rita Rio

Next to me is a radiator
fluting steam. It is my friend
and I call it Rita Rio.
I have painted her day-glo
and I have placed a black light
in my mouth so that when I talk
to her she lights all up.

It is hard to screw her though.
Sometimes she's too hot.
And sometimes she's too cold.
But mostly she's just right.
I use a wool rubber.

At night, especially at three a.m.
when the beer's all out
I put cheeze and crackers
under her tits
and in the morning they are gone.
Rita has nice tits

and sometimes I eat them.
They are nice.

But most of all I like her soul.
She has mystery, a perfect woman
who always loves me.
She has her moods,
but I can take them.
She is all I have
and I love her through the night.

The Fable of the Airplanes

Sometimes when I look in the mirror over the
                                        breakfast table
I think I'm invisible. I think this when
I am alone and not working on my airplane models. But
I do not look in the mirror when this happens. It is
all I have and my wife would laugh at me if I told
her I thought I could disappear but couldnt afterall.

She's at the store now buying some glue for my airplanes.
I have built more than a hundred and they are all an inch
long and half an inch high. My wife is keeping them though.
I am afraid to look for them, since she told me I better not.
I asked her if she was so quiet she wanted a divorce
but she only smiled and took the airplane I had
                                        just finished
and put it with the pile.

We had a child who used to like my toy airplanes
but he was put away when he was three
and we havent seen him since. The doctor said
we will have to put him up for adoption and when
we told him we wanted him back he said no, that
                                        he had proof

of something.

My wife will be home soon and will bring the sausage and
orange juice we will have for supper. I am so hungry but
I'm not supposed to go into the kitchen until
                                          she gets back.
It is a rule. I used to feel it was a stupid rule
but one day I sure found out it wasnt. I went in
there and saw her come out of the mirror that
hangs over the breakfast table with one of my
airplanes crushed in her fist.

The Way It Is

It is not human to make demands on other people.
My wife should know this but she doesn't. She comes
to me while I am sleeping with a hollowed-out television
over her head and screams "Kneel!" and makes me
bow to her life as a television personality. And on into
the night screaming "Banzai!" until I contort
                                          myself into
a small island in the Pacific on which she is marooned
and where the water is rising fast and on until
I turn myself into a dashing lieutenant in the
                                          Coast Guard
who saves her and later ravishes her on the ship,
which is my left leg.

I do not understand my wife, but she has told me
it is not my privilege to question her. She has even
said that this is her love for me, that she loves me very
much, and cries sometimes that I will leave her, even
as she is standing on my body in a pair of snow-skis
pretending I am a mountain slope, and screaming "Fore!"
I have razor rasps, but these are the things that make
our marriage work, she says.

6

I have seen a psychiatrist about all this but he
only stares at the wall and says, "You and your wife
are acting out, which is very good." And then he laughs
and says he will see me next week and rings a little bell
hanging from a bust of Freud's nose. But he does not know
that I am playing his game all along, even as I play
this game with my wife, and one day while all four
of us are in his office, as my wife is screaming "Chink!"
and is laying railroad ties across me, and as he is dying
with excitement and is hitting his little bell with rapid
movements of his left fist, I am going to leave the office
and move to some distant place
where they will never hear from me again.

LYNN SUKENICK

Early Ella

Her voice
slips through our ears
like your arm through mine.

She is the net,
the fish,
and the water.

She sings like women
            swimming,
a bell inside her
            dipping,
            gonging,
like a buoy.

The Poster

1.
He does not have the experience
which is in his poems.
He'll compete
under any conditions.
He is wanted by more women than any other man,
for the mustache
hidden in his mustache.
He gets away with it.
He goes by the name of "Winner."
Watch out for him.

2.
He speaks to me with his knuckles
on my head.
He tells me I am boring.

He hollows out a space inside my chest
as a whittler would do it,
carefully, coolly,
whistling a tune
everyone knows and likes.
He ties up my body
to be shipped somewhere
in a heavy string
and greasy brown butcherpaper.
He is blond
as a nazi.
Each time he looks at me with his frosty eyes,
an animal dies in the local forest
and someone puts on a uniform.

PHILIP DACEY

Chain Letter

Enclosed you will find the names
of every woman you have ever loved
and never stopped loving.
Write a letter to each of them
telling them so. They will not believe it.
Send along a photograph of yourself
in which you cannot be found:
say, This is what it has come to.
Tell them to observe your handwriting,
how—surprising for a man your age—
it wanders erratically like
some river on an old, faded map.
Lastly, remind them of the desperation
of chain letters, how the man who
gives his heart to the mails
always fears it will be returned
stamped, "Sender non-existent."
With your letters to the women
enclose a long list of names,
each of them yours.
Tell them the names need only be
spoken aloud when they're alone
or, when they lie with their loves,
to themselves, softly.
That will preserve the chain.
For your part, if you break the chain,
women you meet will look at you
as if you were a package, ticking,
they had just received.
If you do not break the chain,
all the women you write to
will come to you in dreams,
as delicate as envelopes
that have never been used,

and as exciting, able
to go anywhere.
Remember—this chain letter is illegal.
If you inform the authorities,
we will have to tell them
there must be some mistake,
how we know you, and how your love
has always been the dead letter
boxes have gone rusty waiting for.

Mystery Baseball

No one knows the man who throws out the season's first ball.
His face has never appeared in the newspapers,
except in crowd scenes, blurred.
Asked his name, he mumbles something
about loneliness,
about the beginnings of hard times.

Each team fields an extra, tenth man.
This is the invisible player,
assigned to no particular position.
Runners edging off base feel a tap on their shoulders,
turn, see no one.
Or a batter, the count against him, will hear whispered
in his ear vague, dark
rumors of his wife, and go down.

Vendors move through the stands
selling unmarked sacks,
never disclosing their contents,
never having been told.
People buy, hoping.

Pitchers stay busy
getting signs.
They are everywhere.

One man rounds third base, pumping hard,
   and is never seen again.
Teammates and relatives wait years at the plate,
   uneasy, fearful.

An outfielder goes for a ball on the warning track.
   He leaps into the air and keeps rising,
      beyond himself, past
      the limp flag.

Days later he is discovered,
   descended, wandering dazed
   in centerfield.

Deep under second base lives an old man,
   bearded, said to be
   a hundred. All through the game,
   players pull at the bills of their caps,
   acknowledging him.

The Rowboat

      The rowboat seems to call
To me tonight. I hear small lake-waves slap
      And rock it like a cradle
On the dark shore below the house, where sleep

      Refuses to come to my bed.
The house is empty of my wife and children,
      Who are gone, she said, for good
This time. And so the rowboat says, Come down.

      I take for my nakedness
A blanket draped around my shoulders and go
      Down through the grove of trees

12

To where the boat's all alive in shadow:

It seems to me a hand
Beckoning, sticking out of the lake's sleeve,
Or now a deep lap spread
Wide like a mother's, and I her suckling love.

I push off, one bare foot
Dry and secure in the boat's dipping bow,
The other shocked by the wet
Cold swirl. It's an awkward way, the only I know.

The small boat eases out,
As if it belonged here, and sits upon
The lake's top like the right-
Ful and resolute heir to the night's throne.

What am I doing here,
The artifice of a blanket thinly disguising
How poor I am, and an oar
In each hand poised as for a purpose? Something

Turns the boat around.
The wind has picked up, wants to take the boat
And me its own way. "Wind,
Is this why I've come here in the dark? To sit

And ponder what you mean?
And, that known, whether you mean good or ill?
Whether I should cut clean
Against the pushing waves, against your will,

By striking so, like this,
Making spray fly, the rowboat dive and lift,
Or whether I should kiss
Your great face tenderly and learn to drift?"

Whatever the wind knows,
It only blows and blows. The pine trees bend
    And bend before such force,
Like saints for whom kneel is a prelude to stand.

    But I am no saint. If
I let go or battle, I am no sainted hero.
    I am the man in rough
Water who could drown in all he doesn't know.

    A loon's call! It's so near
It startles me. I search the dark and see,
    Skimming across the water
And making a great fuss, a male loon up to

    His old tricks: three other loons,
A female and two chicks, are swimming the other way,
    And the protective father means
To distract me. I let myself be led astray.

    I see the house beyond
The trees and stroke and stroke again to get there.
    That's the decision: the wind
Won't push me where it will. I'll go counter.

    Yet I know that solves nothing.
Direction, says the loon, can be misdirection:
    I think of me moving
One way upon this lake, my wife and children

    Moving another way
Upon some road, and I know I can't say who's
    Going where, or why.
I only say: I row, and believe I choose.

The Rise and Fall

The rise and fall
at the chest
of an animal.
There is patience
buried near some bellows

begun with time.
A continuing, precisely
right rhythm.
Thought has never
known such slow

steps:
the dance inside
caves of bone,
inhuman
repetitions

of love.
Still they move
with such surpassing
violence,
and explain

nothing.
Translate them!
Translate
the raised hoof.
Read me their story.

Form Rejection Letter

We are sorry we cannot use the enclosed.
We are returning it to you.
We do not mean to imply anything by this.

15

We would prefer not to be pinned down about this matter.
But we are not keeping–cannot, will not keep–
    what you sent us.
We did receive it, though, and our returning it to you
    is a sign of that.
It was not that we minded your sending it to us
    unasked.
      That is happening all the time, they
          come when we least expect them
          when we may not need them,
          when we forget we have needed or might
                        yet need them,
      and we send them back.
We send this back.
It is not that we minded.
At another time, there is no telling...
But this time, it does not suit our present needs.

We wish to make it clear it was not easy receiving it.
It came so encumbered.
And we are busy here.
We did not feel
    we could take it on.
We know it would not have ended there.
It would have led to this, and that.
We know about these things.
It is why we are here.
We wait for it. We recognize it when it comes.
Regretfully, this form letter does not allow us to elaborate
    why we send it back.
We send it back.
It is not that we minded.

We hope this does not discourage you. But we would not
    want to encourage you falsely.
It requires delicate handling, at this end.
If we had offered it to you,
    perhaps you would understand.
    But, of course, we did not.

You cannot know what your offering it
   meant to us,
And we cannot tell you:
there is a form we must adhere to.
It is better for everyone that we use this form.

As to what you do in future,
we hope we have given you signs,
that you have read them,
that you have not misread them.
We wish we could be more helpful.
But we are busy.
We are busy returning so much.
We cannot keep it.
It all comes so encumbered.
And there is no one here to help.
Our enterprise is a small one.
We are thinking of expanding.
We hope you will send something.

Anniversary

Five years.
The wooden anniversary.
We like wood, believe it's
trustworthy.

You have this thing for trees.
Phallic, maybe, but
I've seen gnarled, branching trees
light your eyes.

And wooden sculpture,
for us, has roots,
is still wet
with under-earth.

Our house will be wood.
We'll grow into it
like living wood ourselves,
branching out with children,

and it will grow
into us, turning us
supple but strong
in storms.

I say this: each anniversary
of our wedding
will amaze us
with its rich smell of wood.

TESS GALLAGHER

The Woman Who Raised Goats

Dear ones, in those days it was otherwise.
I was suited more to an obedience
of windows. If anyone had asked,
I would have said: "Windows are my prologue."

My father worked on the docks
in a cold little harbor, unhappily
dedicated to what was needed
by the next and further
harbors. My brothers
succeeded him in this, but when I,
in that town's forsaken luster, offered myself,
the old men in the hiring hall creeled
back in their chairs, fanning themselves
with their cards, with their gloves.
"Saucey," they said. "She's saucey!"

Denial, O my senators,
takes a random shape. The matter
drove me to wearing
a fedora. Soon, the gowns, the amiable
forgeries: a powdery sailor, the blue silk
pillow given by a great aunt, my name
embroidered on it like a ship, the stitched
horse too, with its red plume and its bird eyes
glowing, glowing. There was the education
of my "sensibilities."

All this is nothing to you.
You have eaten my only dress, and the town
drifts every day now
toward the harbor. But always,
above the town, above
the harbor, there is the town,

19

the harbor, the caves and hollows
when the cargo of lights
is gone.

A Poem In Translation

After years smuggling poems
out of an unknown country
you have been discovered by a known
and skillful master. Your language
is foreign and eligible, your circumstances
Russian, complete with prison camps
and midnight journeys by train
through the Urals. Someone is always taking
your hand as a stranger, entrusting you
with a few saved belongings
before he is led away.

You too are led, a pair of eyes
wearing sight like an armor.
You witness it all. You do not suffer
the physical shame, your clothes
taken from you, your body
made to stand with the weeping others.
Somehow you are not harmed.
You stitch a cry into the hem of your coat
to be unraveled in a land of comfort.

They work over the lines like a corpse
taken from the ground. Gradually
they heap their own flesh
over what has remained,
the beautiful gaps and silences.

In the new language you are awkward.
You don't agree with yourself,
these versions of what you meant

to say. Like a journalist, one has written
"throat" where you have said
"throat". Another uses his ears
as a mouth; he writes like an orator
in a bathroom, not "tears"
but "sobbing".

Still another has only heard your name
and the title of one poem
full of proper names, rivers
and cities no one bothers
to translate. All his poems begin here
and move into the dream of you
as the ideal sacrifice, redeeming him
from a language he knows too well
to say anything simply.

One night (it always happens at night)
these translations, against all precautions,
are smuggled back to you by a woman
looking much like yourself. She
takes your hand and leads you away
into a room where each one calls you
by his name and you enter the solitary
kingdom of your face.

Rhododendrons

Like porches they trust their attachments,
or seem to, the road and the trees
leaving them open from both sides.
I have admired their spirit,
wild-headed women of the roadside,
how exclusion is only something glimpsed,
the locomotive dream that learns to go on
without caring for the landscape.

There is a spine in the soil
I have not praised enough:
its underhair of surface
clawed to the air. Elsewhere each shore
recommends an ease of boats, shoulders
nodding over salmon
who cross this sky with our faces

I was justifying my confusion
the last time we walked this way.
I think I said some survivals need
a forest. But it was only the sound
of knowing. Assumptions
about roots put down like a deeper foot
seemed dangerous too.

These were flowers you did not cut,
iris and mums a kindness enough.
Some idea of relative dignities, I suppose,
let us spare each other; I came away
with your secret consent and this
lets you stand like a grief
telling itself over and over.

Even grief has instructions,
like the boats gathering light
from the water and the separate
extensions of the roots. So remembering
is only one more way of being alone
when the voice has gone everywhere
in the dusk of the porches
looking for the last thing to say.

Time Lapse With Tulips

That kiss meant to sear my heart forever—
it went right by.
And the way we walked out on Sundays
to the bakery like a very old couple, arm on
arm, that's gone too
though the street had a house with a harp
in the window.

Those tulips think if they keep being given away
by the black-haired man at our wedding
I'll finally take them in time
for the photograph. They're wrong. This time
I'll hand them back or leave
them sitting in the mason jar
on the grass beside you.

The guests lean after me, their mouths
slightly open. Only now we see
they were never sure, that the picture
holding us all preserves
a symmetry of doubt with us
at the center, the pledge of tulips
red against my dress.

The picture says it is wrong.
I take my image back, the white
petals that were standing a while
at your side, petals falling
a while at your side. Here instead
the trick of flesh held again to your cheek.
Inside, the rare bone of my hand
and that harp seen through a window suddenly

so tempting you must rush into that closed room,
you must tear your fingers across it.

GARY MIRANDA

The One That Got Away

Man, you got a bird where your brain
should be, he says, talking to me.
I say: Perhaps you'd like to explain
that figure of speech for the whole class.

He says: A bird, man, a bird—thass
one o' them things with wings what flies
around. You you jes sits on your ass,
but your brain it flies around, goes

flap an' flap—like this. He shows
me then with his arms, doing flap-an-flaps
between the aisles like a trained crow's
bad imitation of a little black

boy flying. Then he flaps to the back
of the room and out the door, free:
free of the class, that doesn't crack
a smile; free of the teacher, who sits

on his ass, a bird where his brain should be.

Sonnet for Salvador
or:
One could do worse than be a Celery King

Of Salvador the Celery King I sing.
Illiterate in Lewiston, he'd wan-
der, so I'm told, into the ladies' john

And, barring ladies, not suspect a thing.
But when it came to celery he was king,
And when he died the Idaho Daily Sun
Said: Salvador The Celery King Moves On.
The celery hung its head, remembering.

Sometimes I think I'll wind down Lewiston Hill
(Where winding up and winding down's the same
Except for purpose), enter past the mill
And, turning to face the crowd, announce my name:
"Gary, the son of Dom the son of Sal-
vador the King, whose throne I've come to claim."

MARGARET GIBSON

Lunes

O melon-bellied (I talk
to my gut) sweet
hibernaculum: it is time
to come undone.
I want to be empty, I want
to be clean as an eye.
I want an immaculate
suicide.

Lunation is exact to day
and second. I never know mine
until it happens: the cells
ring like wound clocks.
Who put the hex on me,
vengeance in the backbone
the doom of shrink and surfeit
Lupercalian fatness,
moon-fruit.

A friend remarks
the primal tides swing in us,
blossom and seed, migration
of wind, sensation
of the turning season
deeply imprinted.
Such harmony, he says,
is perfect.

Screw perfection.
I'm a slave.
I'd rather be lacuna,
the breaking point in chaos
the zero, primal whore who
all by herself conceived

(to begin with)
perfection
      then time
           then light
                 then word
                 then love
and murder, murder
          then man
             then me.

Apples

I am peeling the apples, making a note to
replenish the cinnamon. The knife pares in
circles. The smell of the peeling teases
the air. I like doing this. I like doing
this alone. When I look out the window the
road stretches back in the distance heavy
with dust. The concord grapes, their bitter
skins are blue. The smell of horses and
stables rises in the air. I am on a fence
rail looking down the road of dust waiting
for what returns after long absences. A
soldier in brown, this man who has always
been missing in action.

I am peeling the apples, making a note that
absence is militant. The peelings huddle
red and white on the table, little slave
bracelets. The man comes down the road,
tracks dust on the carpet. The man is the
knife that whistles at the core. I am
Durer carving the horsemen, hunger history
ceremony rape. I put the bracelets on my
arms. I whistle. White wedges of apple

27

bake in the oven. Death is the heat. I
will sugar them, glaze them, serve them,
and eat.

A Grammar of the Soul

"—while we sleep here, we
are awake elsewhere..."
Jorge Luis Borges

While I am on the dark bus and the spin of the wheels
    carries me into the crowded tunnel

she is rigid awake under the scream of mosquitoes
    and one lightbulb bare in its socket

While I am sleeping in a sling between two palm trees
    which rattle in the trade wind off Cayman

she is hosing the blood off the sidewalks in New York
    after the accident dreaming it green

While I am sleeping in a field of grass making love
    with you so that she will love me

she is in the mirror where it is snowing
    she is freezing to death

When I am unbuttoned in the cold winds of the hailstorm
    or blacked out in the cone of the twister

she pours a glass of cold milk and leaves it
    for me on the kitchen table

When I am dreaming that my body is pacing in the rain alone
    and drifting in the cupboard of a strange city

she walks down the other side of the street wet and

smiling She does not see me when I wave

She does not hear me when I call out for her to stop
    to tell me the name of the city

She cuts through the alley and enters the keyholes
    for she is wiser than I with secrets

While I am sleeping hard with my back turned
    she is writing a poem in my voice

She is lying behind me tracing words on my skin words
    which I will not remember in the morning

When I am pretending to sleep my breathing a snare
    she tacks off on a reach the jib sheet in her teeth

and thinks of heading south to a country where red
    chickens strut in the villages

When she is in the marketplace where the rabbits hang
    by their ears among strings of red pepper and garlic

I whisper how I have always been the stranger here asleep
    in your arms restless and content

When she is sleeping with her maps and charts and lakes
    smoothed over her for cover

I am walking into the room where you are
    drumming your fingers on the polished table

While she sleeps waiting for me to leave you
    I decide to stay

Octobering

When you left I made
my way back to bed
and tried to sleep.

It took a long time
to get there
and my feet were cold.

Outside the wind was loose
with leaves. I put
my arms around myself

and I remembered how
you held me on the floor
and rocked me like a child

until I was one
swinging in the plum
tree of a thin spring

and my body was no longer
my own. That must be
what tenderness is.

In the wind the southing
birds flew out of nowhere,
filled a tree. The green mouth

sang and the birds rose south
again. Touch is a talisman
to take with you as you go.

I am no place now
and the arms around me
are not mine.

I sleep as water does

at the bottom
of a beaded pitcher.

2

Here
where she dropped me
the land of the ledge
me of the head hungover
singing sorry songs
the way a sad man will
when cast among the outlaws
the ones that love forgot
the last ones to be kissed and caressed
Where do we go
in our last parade
into ourselves
searching for solutions in the familiar
Why, why
why did she leave me
impenetrable jungle
vines around my heart like fences
one more sharing
would tear me apart
so I cling to my solitude
a desperate branch
afraid to fall
in love
in a tight heap
with the deep breath of touch held around me
time to cry and cry
while I tear in painful two
each half fighting for parts
Goodbye my heart walk away
away
the leg
in the middle
is mine
alone
to give

Our stars, ourselves
planet bums
captive souls
dried out dreams
cracked, parched blowing into dust
lips split, chapped to peeling red grins
pain is in my heart
it is time to say goodbye
head spinning
dizzy darling
mirror running
head on face to face
with this mascara'd meter
time is up time isup timeisup
crash I came
bang I'm alive no more
we were because we are not now
in time
some atom thrusting
lust up yes
space gasp yes
ooh yes
sun up over nature's pulsing thighs
shooting stars
we felt the universe tremble
in the hard night falling
life a crystal ball
the future is in our hands
our hands are in the air
surrender is on our minds
the air is in our heads
the stars are in our eyes

No one is as acquainted with pain as I am
I know its music
every note of anguish
in every key and variation
I
can rock it
as I suffer its slow acid dance
feeling it stick and burn
slithering scalding
boiling syrup
through my heart
through my fingers
I hear its tune now by this river
moon watching blank
its slick cataract eye
on the murky film
as I stumble toward the end of my life
pain, the moon, and old love
sinking with my dreams
in the muddy water
the river ripples like a soft stomach
the sucking slap of the waves
calls to me
a woman's huge and flooded sex

there were once giants in this land
boisterous booming voices
blood beneath their feet
wrath blackening the sky
marching like thunder over the insect world
I ask the old ones
do they miss them?
now that they are gone
when small things seem so dear
they never answer
they say now that I'm big time

and I have crowds dancing in the aisles
instead of running
hands to head
to homes in flames
crushed with tear-streaked faces

the peasants' hearts
just rock now
to a beat
oh so
they think
safe
the people's pet
I play
they dance
to music of this midget band
but when I lead
I sneak them some of the old tunes
make them move in the little dance of anguish
but even I can't make the big notes all alone
no colossal pain
just a tear
here, there
shake an ass now
when they used to shake
their lives
becoming frantic dancers all
horror stained, frenzied trancers
drenched in a giant's blood
with an army's raining glory
but now
they'd rather pat their feet
than step out fighting
with their tiny hearts
they will miss their crush
when I have released them
from my dreams
from their dancing to their weight
from their last chance

at a death of glory
by a giant's hand

CHARLOTTE ALEXANDER

The Write-Off

Brian never makes a real fire
when he gets home;
Brian turns on the electric bar and pays more.

Brian is getting over something,
slowly.

Brian eats fry too often.

Brian (apparently) wanted (briefly) to die
on Christmas Eve,
the road between his daughter and him
stringing
like hot red Christmas ribbon,
teasing him too near
the Christmas beer and whiskey in his brain.

(Who is to say what sane means?
Cherish the friend who slipped by
that lonesome Christmas ride
and rescued Bri.)

Brian may be better now,
some home cooked dinners past his belly,
and wearing his suit on Fridays.

Brian can drive very well
(though the wreck of his car doesn't show it:
a write-off).

Brian brought candy, like my old man used to do.
Brian bought papers, cigarettes and magazines
for the train.

And furthermore, Brian makes a damn good fire,
though he doesn't quite yet know it.
Brian is due for a lovely change.

Brian, lady, is no longer for hire.

JOHN SKOYLES

This Business of Dying

I don't care at all who died today.
There's not a single reason
to list the deaths today.
Maybe my father opens the sports page
or my mother a mystery novel
in New York this afternoon,
a place where on another day
I could follow death like a woman
into the subway, where death
is just a headline, where boys
light freezing derelicts on fire.

So let's forget who died today,
the families, their keepsakes, the clumsy last breaths.
Because this afternoon I know
I've invested my heart in good places,
that if this woman drops off to sleep
right now I'll still be here exhaling,
feeling guilty but lucky,
like a man with no connections.

Because everyone left for work today
loving their children but cursing their lives.
Some union men, on strike again,
lounged in taverns,
lost count of their beers
as I've lost count of these hours,
this afternoon, the days I've run through,
and the woman who moved me
this far, so far from my death.

Evidence

I used to pray in furnished rooms,
rooms where only my conscience
waited up when I came in late;
but since I'm with this woman
I hardly ever pray; I think of my childhood,
my parents back home; and maybe raising
a daughter like the woman beside me,
and I remember what it's like
to live alone, with nothing but fantasy,

and what living with a woman's like,
with its special loneliness,
and the two lives not that far apart,
like this world and the next:
men and women with no place to go
make God less alone, and couples
walk the same streets as the homeless,
both having someone to point to
when asked what they did with their lives.

No Thank You

Who'll be the lover of that woman on the bench?
If she wants to hurt someone, she can use me.

Did she mean it, or was she trying to be unforgettable?
If she wants to use someone, she can hurt me.

I'll use my manners to stay in one piece,
but I wind up believing every excuse that I make.

I always sigh when I see a woman like this;
I don't know where it comes from and I don't know
                                where it goes.

I thought I'd enjoy a beautiful day like today;
I took a walk in the park and then something
like this happens.

GERARD MALANGA

The Insistence

We are as we find out we are —*Charles Olson*

There's one leaf in the birchwoods that's shining
and it's talking to me —
an echo that's frozen
because it takes in the pain

I pass it each day
if i go back to where
i think it is
i may never find it

like the shadow
searching pockets
for its hands
the body, then, is where I am

so tired it wants to fall apart
the body is screaming
the body wants out
where shall I begin

Inside the dream there are sounds waking up
poems rush in and out of a darkness
the half-heard voices of night growing more faint
the phone rings or it doesn't

there was no one there
when I woke
Suddenly I am following the sun in this journey
                                    through darkness
suddenly I know my way around in this darkness

CHARLES CANTRELL

Aladdin's Lamp

On a stiff morning I raise the greasy shade and see the magic
of morning glories opening after last night's shower, and a
redwing blackbird shitting on my Chevy. I discover maggots
beneath the crust of my Cheshire's salmon cat food.

I think: grape mouth why not let a fly graze on your lips?
That's the real kiss, the real high, with the possibility
of a magic act.

Later, munching a strip of bacon, I patrol with binoculars
the backyard fence like a silent dog on a civilized leash.
My finger points over the camouflaged sheets
                                        harboring room,
love, and sometimes. . . shame.

Cat out, I walk the rainy block flattening earth-
                              worms. Tough
trees, slicked down... free weeds, at stud... My dry shadow
sucks my soaked heels. What violence brews in
                              the religious
distance between us... strolling lovers? I purge this thought
by staring at a waterlogged newspaper containing
                              arranged ac-
cidents occurring in mild weather or perfect beds.

Lunch with father, loosening belts; after cock-
                              tails and stories
he dozes, and the tiny glacier slide of the vodka cubes start-
les him. He spills the funny papers on his spaniel, and shivers
as if tied down at the bottom of an ice avalanche. "Turn the
heat up," he says. "And take your Grandma her lunch."

Cobwebs grow thick in the coffee cups hung from
                              pegs in Grand-

43

ma's clapboard house. In the breeze, whiffs of
kerosene from
the kitchen lamp where light was so thick we could spoon it
up like sugar, while she read fables at bedtime. Aladdin's
lamp, I called it, Aladdin's lamp.

The Amputee

Amputation numbs with its cold logic.

His hands crawl away
like five-pointed stars
aching toward a corner of the galaxy.

His ears fly off
like sand dollars
inflating the ocean by one ounce.

His feet are dropped to the bottom
of a lake on a block of cement
and become an idol for fish.

Both legs, auctioned at the hospital,
are stored in a deep freeze with cats and steaks.
The cannibalism is clear,
but the cat's origin is a mystery.

Both arms, bulging with muscle,
one with a "Mother" tatoo
are launched into space
tagged: These are Earthling arms.

A lump of clay, his torso
pulsates beneath the rhythm of dreams.

In one he is a meteor
flying toward Mars

with no apparent mission.

In another someone draws
the hands of a clock with cold paint
upon his chest, and stamps:
Keep in a cool place on his forehead.

Before waking, he rolls toward a hole
covered with green felt,
and discovers he is a billiard ball.
Falling down the pocket
gives him an erection.

When he wakes, a nurse is attempting
to remove his moist underwear.
Another is standing like a soldier
armed with brush and toothpaste.

The amputee smiles like a weasel full of eggs.

MARIE HARRIS

from INTERSTATE

Leaving Ithaca: Buttermilk Falls
or the deep pool in Six Mile Creek where I swam,
shedding a day of late spring with my shirt and jeans,
squatted naked on the warm rocks with a few quiet friends:

leaving with my children north to Toronto
(north on I-89
west on 90 to Buffalo and across an international boundary
where even the names of the hamburger stands don't change

three of us an our essentials

> tape recorder full of music
> 2000 baseball trading cards
> hiking boots and sweaters
> typewriter

you learn
what to carry around with you

> now we are just three of the hundreds
on our way toward the Calgary Stampede, reluctant, excite
fragile

aboard CNRR coach
settled and moving
out of Toronto, I imagine
hands at every smudged window
knocking for my attention
writing desperate messages on the dusty glass
"Don't go! It's the same
everywhere!"

> monarch butterflies

                              counting the distance
                              in short meter
                              from pole to pole until
                              they speed by too fast

north by Georgian Bay turning dark ....Sudbury
west
to the Soo

                              we sleep sitting up
                              slumping on each other

Thunder Bay... people
get off there
giving us more room

                              Thunder Bay: titles
                              off library books
                              I used to read—
                              magic beyond the
                              reality of smokestacks

Kenora... Irish fog rising off the lakes
look way out the train window and see the end of the train
emerging from a forest, the engine ahead turning through
a forest

Manitoba-Saskatchewan...Winnipeg at midnight, like any
station at midnight: a rush for Hershey bars and magazines.
Standing on one foot, then the other wondering about
Winnipeg
              or
                   Regina, Moose Jaw, Swift Current
morning approaching Medicine Hat, Alberta
(meanwhile we pass the time train-fashion, eating
                                        and visiting,
walking like sailors)

Crossed the whole continent carrying the children
like saddlebags

when I dashed off the train for fresh bread
and cheese
they hung out the window, yelling
as the conductor announced the minutes
till departure   schooled in departures,
we adapt to counting backwards

Calgary, Alberta, CANADA

South on Rt 2 by car to Fort McLeod
west on Rt 3 over Crow's Nest Pass B.C. to Fernie

(stopped for a few minutes at Frank Slide, marveling at
where all that rock came from
                              so fast
what it takes to bury a town
                              instantly)

TO: my next sister's home FROM: Ithaca, Buttermilk Falls
and the deep pool in Six Mile Creek where I swam, shedding
a day of late, indoor spring with my jeans and shirt, squatting
naked with a few
quiet friends.

TO: Anny, my next sister FROM: Ithaca, Buttermilk Falls
a marriage of ten years

we make space for each other, pushing aside
a half-finished peanut butter and jelly sandwich,
a pile of newspaper, layer on layer
travelling the miles of Interstate, the years of exits,
birthdays, children's birthdays

To Anny for a month in the Canadian Rockies
(the sky is a foggy weight-belt on the Three Sisters, rain
like a mud boot on the valley, the bush is rain
and river)

                        Tango fell in love with me and I
                        fell in love with his
horses
salt lick
bighorn sheep

when you move around a lot you mistake sentiment
for home

mistake jealousy for love
separation for love
habit for love
children for love

Dear Anny:
                (and we write disjointed letters to each other

            * * * * * * * * * * * * *

We live with our mistakes
for 17 miles to the next exit
the silence between us brims so easily to anger

each headlight cuts the fog at a different angle
the thin clouds arrange themselves against a giant moon
in the image of a fish skeleton

                            staying awake
fighting back
the temptation to sleep
Gethsemane

knowing it will begin again in the morning, craving
sleep's healing deception

the missed exit another accident
in the perpetual accident of our lives
together

REST AREA
in which
(clean, machined, 24 hr)
I might
at another time
rest

* * * * * * * * * * * * *

we came when there were no more horses
and played in the stables and left at night before the arrival
of the groom ghosts

we came when there were no more swimmers from the
World's Fair   we constructed elaborate dances in the pool
we theorized on the effects of chlorine watched each other
hoping one of us would turn blue

we came there after the nights of candles that
lined the gravel drives   after the dances   before
the hurricane

we came with the surviving nannies
we were the blond seersucker aboriginals
the last of a short line from Ireland to suburbia

on the way down there were towns
called An Hour Away

Almost There   roads named The Fastest Way and Sunrise

to the summer internment camp
for women and children
bounded by sculptured hedges patrolled by Irish
guards with day uniforms and night uniforms
silver artillery
bone china charts
cut flowers
marble backgammon board
a chapel of slipcovers and second-best
stations of the cross
summer clergy in sportshirts

we were the cousins
we were the shorebirds

the smell of salt
the hunched pine and beachrose
swans
undertow

what there was to do with a day wouldn't fill
a day now

grandfather made speeches out of atomic particles
like sparklers on the fourth of July that stayed lit

Margot had boyfriends
I had a diary and tacks
and a boyfriend called Stevie who died later

we turned brown as the rotogravure

:this is my love song to the ocean:

we were the last children

monogrammed pieces of the place were found

eighteen miles down the coast after the hurricane

* * * * * * * * * * * * *

you imagined the lover I will never be I am
so sorry

tripping on the hem of it
falling backward
into the bottomless apology I am
so sorry:

like that
the fog shreds the edges of the horned moon
and yesterday's sharp snowfall

the road home
is a short memory
I reinvent ahead of the low beams

* * * * * * * * * * * * *

now it's my mother
who's moving
                    she worries for me in her dreams

moving! it must be
like ripping
the tree-climbing tree
out of the ground in winter: she may take
all of her land with her
held together by roots
                    a piece of the ground
                    and a piece of the frozen sky

when my mother hits the road
with her remaining children and little left
                    I stay up late

                         waiting for a phone call
                         saying she's arrived

                                        safely, my
                                        daughter

                    * * * * * * * * * * * * *

we leave layers of ourselves
dried and unrecognizable in schoolyards
and emptied rooms
the skins are patterned
they can be read like a snakeskin
a severed tree
a caterpillar
a riverbed
they can be preserved on a windowsill

I have lost Jane
the way one loses
a cousin to Europe or Mexico

Cynthia has wandered back to a new weather
we keep our distance in keeping
with how it started

Colette rides the Long Island RR
bolstering our faltering faith in transportation
that brings us there
and home
over and over

the molting is one kind of record
transparencies we hold up to the light
to remember that summer that move that terror
of being alone

sometimes it's all we have left
the stiff skin of a friendship

layer on layer
we build a delicate road
that shatters concrete without disturbing
the rootsystem
of the marsh marigold

* * * * * * * * * * * * *

I-93

the completion of the stretch
between here and the border
is in doubt

I am camped in the shadow of the earth
movers

RUDY SHACKELFORD

Entreaties

I went to the prince of nettles
and bowing before him
implored a crumb of pain

he said You are not worthy
to suffer Go stare
at the sun

but the sun had gone
into an unscheduled eclipse

I waited years at the drawbridge
for a ship which was never to pass

the harborman beckoned me Leap!
had I trusted him
I wouldn't be drowning there in the sand

to the keeper of the bell tower
I ascended
the iron spiral of his inner ear

he stood draped in ropes
studying a table of changes

One spends a lifetime here
he said Preparing to ring the hour

ALAN ZIEGLER

Displacement

You come home,
find your possessions gone,
you sigh
and go to bed.

Awakening abruptly,
you find your bed gone,
stolen from under your nose.
So tired,
you go back to sleep.
You'll investigate later.

You re-awake
to a slap of chill wind.
Someone has made off with the south wall.
Back to sleep,
overcoat on blanket.

You dream
of walking off to distant places.
When you wake again
you are a double amputee.

By morning
there is no
trace of you.

Waiting for the Bus

This small town bus station has its own drunk. Buses
pull in all day and night, but he has never taken one.
Everyone knows him but no one talks to him. His only

needs seem to be a bottle of whiskey and a brown paper bag to drink it from. One could say he is tolerated.

One night a shiny new bus marked SPECIAL pulls in. The puzzled station manager re-checks his schedule—there are no charters due. The drunk looks up, flashes the smile his mother loved him for, takes a swig, and walks toward the loading gate. On the way he opens an unlocked 25-cent locker and takes out a large paper bag.

The bus driver nods and the drunk boards the bus without handing him a ticket. The bus is full of drunks—singing, "A million bottles of beer on the wall, a million bottles of beer..." The bus roars off; I feel like I have just watched a close friend leave.

I come back the next night and stare at the seat vacated by our drunk. He doesn't show up. I come every night, but he doesn't return. I start drinking to pass the waiting-time away, and rarely shave. People stop talking to me.

Till one night the bus marked SPECIAL comes back. I nervously enter. The bus is quiet; they look me over. As we pull away, I shyly pass my bottle around, then everyone breaks out singing, "650,568 bottles of beer on the wall, 650,568 bottles of beer..."

The drunk from my town takes me under his wings. They take to calling me "the kid"—when we stop for gas I run in for sandwiches and beer. "Bring us something nice, kid," is what they say.

We wind up out West in a ghost town with many saloons, all fully stocked and free. Saloons and bus stations galore this town has, also pool halls and hotel lobbies. Town meetings are held in the old stagecoach waiting room. The bus goes out occasionally and brings back more immigrants with brown paper bags. Soon the town is full.

Tourist buses start showing up, but we send them away. People come in cars loaded down with baggages, pulling U-Hauls full of furniture. We politely tell them to turn back. "We didn't know," they say. "We just didn't know."

Sunday Night

You go outside
carrying the remains
of a wretched weekend
wrapped in a large brown paper bag
dripping bacon grease
brimming with tin cans half full
of concentrated soup
stuffed with crumpled papers

A crazed dog challenges you
for your garbage
you resist
though you certainly have no use for it
you want the dog
to ask you nicely
whimper and perhaps even heel
you hold your ground

It is not enough that you refuse
his uncocked mouth
that you stand pat against his damp snarling
you hold the bag out to him
and kick his horny mouth

Now the dog is berserk
with hunger and anger
the rancid smorgasbord you clutch
will no longer satisfy him
it's a piece of you he wants
he salvages your weekend
the way he looks at you
the way no one has looked at you
for so long

Curtain Call

They signed to play the leading man and leading lady in a two-character production. They had so much trouble learning their lines, they decided to move right on to the set and rehearse constantly. Once they began to get the script down, everything was nearly perfect for them there; they knew what to expect at all times. Yes, there were forgotten lines, but improvising could be interesting fun sometimes, and offstage whispers would soon get them back on the track. They were so compatible, and they often—to themselves, before they went to sleep—thanked the Author that this wasn't one of those "relevant" plays about isolation and betrayal. No, a light drawing room comedy. It did have its rough spots, yes, but nothing that wasn't dealt with: a misunderstanding or two that would put them in doubt, but soon cleared up; and a couple of pratfalls (which practice made safe). By and large, it was a pleasant little thing, to be breezed through. There were no emotional standing ovations to be had, but neither were there any jeers or tears from the audience. Tears on stage were difficult enough for them (and there were a few drops in this production), but sobs from the audience had always been totally disagreeable.

***

They live there day and night; they are pros and it doesn't matter if the house is full or empty. At three in the morning, the night watchman sometimes hears them going through a scene: "I'll be off now, see you in three weeks," he might say. "I'll miss you," she would reply, winter or summer, knowing he'll be back in the time it takes the curtain to go down and back up.

***

It is a long-running hit; people keep coming back. But the actors gradually grow old and tired, so agree to make it a movie.

"Cut!" the director yells on the last day of filming. "Print it!"

Now they spend their days and nights on the empty stage, sitting behind the whirring projector, slipping each other winks and smiles. Ideal companions in the perfect marriage. Till one tragic day, the fever comes and she is gone. He is left to stare alone at the lights flashing on the screen. He shuts off this Past Machine. "I am too old for auditions and rehearsals," he thinks. He begins to cry. The sobs reach out into the empty theater and their echoes reverberate between the orchestra seats and the walls of the bare stage. In the darkened theater, they sound to him like the whole audience is sobbing.

The Guest

I am lost and knock on the nearest door to ask directions. There's a crowd, a party going on. I'm about to apologize for interrupting, but everyone at the party treats me as if my arrival has been highly anticipated, though I'm sure I'm here by accident. This woman embracing me—do I know her? And this man who slaps my back—is he an old roommate from school? They are listening to the music I like best, and offer me shrimp with lobster sauce, my favorite. Is this in my honor? Did I do something worthy without being aware of it? I decide to relax and enjoy it; why analyze and maybe spoil it? I sit back, and one by one they come to me. "It was nothing," I hear myself saying— at least I am telling the truth. Later, a teary woman makes her way through the crowd. She calls me inconsiderate and curses at me. I don't know how to respond, so I say nothing. Then she leaves, and everyone is quiet. The host comes over and says softly with a tinge of bitterness, "You know, you shouldn't have ignored her all night. It was hard enough for her to come. Sometimes you can be such a bastard."

JOHN MORGAN

The Psychoanalysis of Fire

Evenings a roach of light scrabbling through
the walls of an hieratic solitude
as the frantic child imagines in procession
twelve cauled and swaying men,
    ghost-like, their torches
spiraling into the cavernous
moss-ridden vaults of the mind.

And by dawn the autumn landscape holds in perspective
flats and vectors, irreconcilable distances
from which the spark of flint is never absent.
The boy gathers leaves, desiring
a paradise of ashes, while from the brow of the sky
a pulsing threatening eye looks down upon the earth
as on a dangerous son.

Toying with matches—see the magnificent havoc,
the wrestling bright bodies of the flame.
Look, as an ember surges and darkens, at the terrible
filial fear of the boy.
    And when the cooling ash dies out of his reverie
his skin's as dry as a snake's, his fingernails singed—
alone and afraid, his darkness shifts under the house.

And this deceitful, beautiful reticence of fire
that wavers deeply into the drowsing night
as a cool blue mist, like the prodigious feat of will
that, in the outlying suburb of the present, can recall
those ancient burning fields, that lurid sky,
where the moon, a calm and loving face,
first went up in flames—

faster and faster, the long abyss of fire
while in his arbitrary fury
—because in the end we are all
lost, all
dancing into ash—he beats against the finiteness
and infancy of time: the child, my dark-eyed son,
may he never be born.

MICHAEL BURKARD

The Victim

Yes, it's all right that the stars are like that, I mean
without much seriousness, without dying. But then
that's what you keep insisting on isn't—seriousness—
like that photograph purchased second hand, you've
forgotten where, that simplifies the gray house, the
old cane chair facing east, blonder in the gray sun than
you might have assumed. And sometimes—if you tip the
photograph toward a near light—the cane chair disappears.
There is no sign of life here, and you must admit that
even in your approach to talking about it this way—the
photograph I mean—there is not much sign of life in that
either, at least not new. You notice in the northern cor-
ner of the house, near the attic, the tree limbs will never
be able to be seen again. It is impossible to tell what
kind of tree this is, and that's no excuse. The curtains
are drawn. Outside your window—here—a yellow leaf
trickles down through the air like a handkerchief would,
say, from a train. A signal in distress. No one pays any
attention. I think I've noticed that there is a large un-
comfortable splotch on the victim's neck, that you had
not seen before. Was that yesterday, was the movement
of the person, dark in the night light, familiar or not?
Was it that simple? Anyway, your attention was petering
out until that moment, that point, and the person aroused
much in you. Like that leaf I mentioned before, the one
that is still dropping. There are many questions. The
refusal of anything to stay still—not even the cane chair
because, as I said, of the way you tilt it toward the light.
Or let's say the shift from the more incomplete landscape
to the more redundant one, how you don't know the
species of the tree, and perhaps, for this one small moment,
were not meant to. Oh and yes, I'm tired of talking about
the terminal point, as you might have guessed, although

63

I have not even begun to talk about it. The entire house is fading out now, and I won't disturb this play of light on it—I'll let it fade for awhile. The person disappears and the signal. The night came down and you went to sleep, and the terminal point became a seriousness reflected in a window of the train, passing for the sake of the victim.

Wren: Three Mirrors

Like waking in the small room, looking out,
seeing the moon, almost down, through the pale
trees. So then the incompletion is waking
also, taking your shoulder and now your hand
beyond the past method, although beyond is also
a quarry. There, by that water which is also
beyond, two black wings turn in their mirror,
the mirror the tree makes above them, and then
break with the incomplete torture of the shade
descending. But it doesn't matter—the woman
walks her attic, reaches the house before you.
Why stop there, why climb through the field
when field was just an attempt to close off
this silence, to close, to say silence I have
missed you like a donkey on fire, like a donkey.

Gaslight
for Isaac Babel

I had to do all that: because
she always felt cold, because my books
were extinguished by a flood of milk.

I endured the loud whip and told the mortar,
go in peace.

Everyone wants a feeding;—imagine,
an axe proposes to the window, the vowels
of the moon in this same place!

September, 1920:
"the fog bled. The barn
temporarily drooped."

Our attendants: a fat professor
who refuses to remove his coat, a girl student
making drawings of the stomach.

Marius, water blackens the metaphor.
You would better confuse the heart with blood.
Such passages are rare . . . the blood large,
decent; flowing behind the window. The occasion
for this is your first pair of glasses.

(Untitled)

If the composition of this collection lasted three years,
didn't she talk? Even if that took place in the rain, during, say,

only two days, during only two hours of the future, two hours
of the rain, didn't she speak? Didn't she have to?

This evening when I go off with myself
I go off with myself. This is a suicide, this going off,

this is a sideways suicide, but I mean to give this to you.
I needed rain, the way in which it would feel itself,

so that when the rain came, as it did this afternoon, I knew
I'd go off to you. When I committed suicide it wasn't easy,

it wasn't easy by any means: everyone I did not know wanted
to talk about it, but their manner of talking about it

was manner, hovering like a plane that didn't land, but
kept believing in itself, as if it would. They also

had a way of leaving me out, even as they talked
they talked as if I had nothing to do with it, my own

suicide, my fallen men and my fallen women which have wept
now here in my body, in the very disparate areas of my body,

for twelve years. I thought it appropriate they left me out,
that they hovered over me, although it angered me
                                        at the same time.

An author's note would say something like this: "five
                                        minutes or so,"
but I am not an author. I think authors are assholes.

And that hesitation is a jealousy that is no better than feeling
sorry, which is no better than the absence of jeal-
                                        ousy finally means.

The author's note says something like we'll finally
                                        meet, in 1950
or in 1976, or for that matter that we won't meet,
                                        like the rain

today and this evening won't meet me, as much as
                                        I would like it to.
I can't hesitate: I don't think the rain is worth coming back to,

I don't think suicide is worth coming back to, and this leads
me to think that the body itself is not worth it either.

This would mean that the mind is in an even worse
                                        place, falling back
like a memory that has no possibility of being remem-
                                        bered. Or it means this:

When I committed suicide you were startled, and
                              at the same time
there was a warm place, a warm place entitled "depar-
                              ture," the way an author

an asshole, would entitle it. And in this distance there
                              is the same kind
of memory as the memory I see that crosses your face, even

from the easy loving that rain was, and will be,
—one evening I will submissively return to this departure,

and I will walk in back of myself, like a shadow will walk,
like a shadow walks now in back of myself. I will disconnect

any old grief you feel, I will take it, I will take it off the wall
like you can take a telephone off the wall, then I will speak

on that phone: authors are assholes, the rain that is lost is
memory that is lost, like you are, and I'll walk,

I will walk in a very local direction, and I will re-
                              venge the change
that memory brings, as it must bring, as it changes,
                              as it must change.

GARY SOTO

Telephoning God

for Jon Veinberg

Drunk in the kitchen, I ring God

And get Wichita,
Agatha drunk and on the bed's edge, undoing
her bra.

Dial again, and Topeka comes through like snoring,
Though no one sleeps. Not little Jennifer
Yelling "But Mommy,"

      nor Ernie kissing
The inside of his wrist, whispering
"This is a Gorgeous Evening."

Dial again, and only the sound of spoons crashing
In a cafeteria in Idaho,

A little silence, then a gnat circling the ear
of Angela beaten and naked in the vineyard,
Her white legs glowing.

The Underground Parking

para J.T.

A man who holds fear
Like the lung a spot of cancer,
Waits for your wife.
He is already listening for her whimper
To stop echoing and to break
Against concrete, listening

For the final fist at her ear,
For morning to arrive
Without the door tearing from its hinges.

The woman who gets it in a car
Or on the hard earth of a vacant lot,
Is under the heaviness of a toilet not flushing,
Of Out of a job and Why change
Bedsheets? She is under arms of tattoos,
Kick in the mouth, shitted shorts,
An ice pick at the throat.
She faces No rent money, Alice,
And not a single tear or a multitude could pull him off.

When his breath sours with fear,
And he cringes at the finger poking the doorbell,
I could give him the bread of my luck
And a prayer to go along—
If your fist closes, open it.
If you curse, swallow your tongue
Because you won't have anything to say,
Not a kind word to lead him
From where he squats, waiting.

Moving Away

Remember that we are moving away   brother
From those years
In the same house with a white stepfather
What troubled him has been forgotten

But what troubled us has settled
Like dirt
In the nests of our knuckles
And cannot be washed away

All those times you woke shivering

In the night
From a coldness I
Could not understand
And cupped a crucifix beneath the covers

All those summers we hoed our yard
In the afternoon sun
The heat waving across our faces
And we waved back wasps
While the one we hated
Watched from under a tree and said nothing

We will remember those moments   brother

And now that we are far
From one another
What I want to speak of
Is the quiet of a room just before daybreak
And you next to me   sleeping

WILLIAM J. HIGGINSON

The Loves and Lays of William J. Higginson

I. And she shall remain nameless

And she shall remain nameless
the girl
     who opened her snowpants
          one blustery day
the year we were five.
        A few dead leaves
          crackling
in new-spring wind
       straggled overhead
          from last autumn
before sex landed in my life.
        I had shown her mine
(Was she impressed?)
      and now sought
        the much
          more interesting
vision of hers.
      Not knowing then
        how far inward
        one must go
seeking love
     I saw nothing
      and said to her
        over and over
till she must have been bored with it:
        I don't see anything.

On Reading Lao-tzu

The cat and I are in love.
His hind claws tear at the tendons of my wrist.

His fore claws raise welts on the back of my hand.
I grab at his fore paws.
He digs deeper into the back of my hand.
I scream GET YOUR CLAWS OUT OF MY HAND!
He sinks teeth into the other hand.
I remove his fore paws from the back of the one hand,
grasp his hind paws with it,
roll him over and bite a large fold of skin at the
                                        back of his skull.
Snarling, I move the hand he is biting so that he
                                        bites his own lip.
He sinks claws into the hand, releases it with his teeth.
Simultaneously, we scream and let go.
He goes under the bed to wash up.
I look under the bed, he glares at me.
I go to the sink to wash up.
He enters the bathroom, I snap a towel at him.
I go to the typewriter to write a poem.
He leaps to the work table next to me.
We touch noses.

Other Woman

1

She knew. The wife's voice,
polite and terrible, hurled steel
curettes, outlining me —
neither quite Fair dummy nor wholly
human, though there were nicks
and blood-runnels. Oh,
that was a bad time.
I had imagined it all too
vividly, cramping, eyeballing
black acrackle at two in the morning;
it was the nightmare, come.
A doomed subtraction
straw by straw of everything it still
might mean instead took days,
and in the end
left only "She smells a rat. Her
talk's too pointed," flat.

2

Curious that exposure largely
should mean relief. Out of that bag,
cat! If this is the death
of us you may as well un-
cramp first, tongue your fur flat,
and see the sun, and let the sun
see you. I'm fagged out, I admit it,
juggling twenty claws in a humping
gunnysack. Damn them,

they pricked through not
like conscience yet
at all the wrong times; times
were all wrong. Another curious
thing though about exposure:
it's lost her her advantage. I mean
somehow she needed me in the dark,
wondering.

3

Decency is left even to those
who have lost everything
else; one can still and always
be kind. Charity may give
shape to our grief and in any case
we three are so like so many
Virginia wounded in a Yankee
field hospital where we ourselves
come or no one does
from cot to cot bringing water
laudanum and lint. And charity
serves also to keep one
busy, which is not beside the point.
All of us are losers, have lost
yes everything but listen:
this
is as far as I go.

SUSAN HARTMAN

In the Generation that Laughed at Me

Sleeping
under the longest root
of the tree,
I waited
for a woman with my face.

The women passed by
on their way to the market.
Chattering under the branches,
they broke off monkey bread,
sucking it as they walked.

Those women knew me
before I lost face
and went underneath the ground.

When I left the village,
they dug holes
near the roots of the tree
and poured palm wine
down to me.

In the generation
that laughed at me,
the woman with my face passed
with her lover. She tripped over a stone,
and as they laughed
I rose through the roots,
slipped into her small body.

Tapping her lover's arm, I ran ahead.
He followed me laughing.
We re-entered the village.

After His Death

At night, the children came into my room
looking for their father.

Not finding him, they fell on me,
loaded me onto their backs.

Their spines cut me through their thin clothes,
their feet dragged, mourning.

As they carried me they pinched my soft legs
and poked my stomach full against their backs.

They cursed me for not having leaned
on a cane and for laughing
before three years had passed.

Reaching a cave, they shifted me
from their backs to their arms.
They crammed my body
no bigger than theirs into its mouth.

They said, "No one can live
in the same house
with the wife of a ghost."

T.E. PORTER

(*The Raft of* The Medusa)

in memory of Howard Jurgrau

I

The whole world disappeared on the first night.
In the dark we sucked the void of dead memory
and a hundred hearts bled bubbles at each pitch
and lift of our groaning, madman's raft.
Black as blindness and nobody dared to sleep:
smell of shark's-breath at every roll she rolled.

But by first light the rising seas rolled
across a craft half unpeopled in the night.
Many at last had gone to sleep.
The rest, still breathing, birthed a new memory
that would wait like the shrouded shapes beneath the raft,
or sit at the backs of minds like pots of pitch

to caulk a leaky life when the time came: The pitch
of the ramshackle planks, we later claimed, rolled
fifty men to the sharks that dogged the raft
more avid than the day was dogged by another night
or half a hundred minds by the new memory.
The only woman we had was the only one to sleep,

for now the men knew reasons not to sleep
as new-formed factions prowled the planks to pitch
the weak and weary into the new memory.
With feeble pleas, gestures, sighs of release, they rolled
off the boards; sometimes a yell leaked through the night,
but nothing could touch the strong ones on the raft.

Nevertheless, with new light, lassitude ruled the raft,

as if, silently, we agreed even the strong need sleep
and so truced, rode stormy day into tranquil night,
the brotherly blood among us thick as pitch,
while on the roiling water our bundle of sticks rolled
on, the sea like a vast mind and we an elusive memory.

On the fourth day, the woman found the new memory
and the new fact that lay like fog upon the raft:
That she was weak, was next to be rolled
in the sea. "I felt you sucking at me in my sleep,"
was all she said. We watched her body pitch
once when the shark struck; then it was night.

The memory and woman washed us in our sleep,
we dreamed the raft was a pool of boiling pitch
where we tossed and rolled and moaned through
                                    the long night.

II

Certain inferences would seem
inescapable: The help
you were counting on
has not arrived; the ports
of every possible convenience
were found later to be mirages;

indeed, your table is furnished
with most unusual fish.
And those irregular flags
that fly in your disordered
rigging... Yet you are
as affable as a needy guest

at a gracious table,
your always wavering interest
having been revived by a conversation
you seem to have overheard before:

"Est-ce-que vous êtes une demi-vierge..."
(in the arms of Death)!

III

and everywhere
are fear, harsh grief and many shapes of slaughter.

By day wrestling the angel of easy death,
by night collapsed amidst the happy corpses
we found the secret of our single heart,
adrift in the truest latitude of being.
By day, by night, sleeping and waking each dreamed
from the single heart, a myriad of the forms of fear.

"By day I lay my ear against the lips of fear,
by night I lay my lips upon the ear of death.
Asleep I asked the dead to tell me what they dreamed,
and waked *a carezza* with the stinking corpses.
I cut their veins to catch the flow of being,
and when they groaned was gracious in my heart,

"and when they howled I ripped them out my heart
to hear it sing equivocal songs of fear.
And felt my veins throb to the threat of being.
Acknowledging then the deft accomplishments of death
I placed my feelings in trust to the corpses.
Aloud, my live companions wondered what I dreamed,

"mocking the words I uttered while I dreamed.
Perverse, I hid my visions in my heart,
discoursed on the numerous discreet parts of corpses,
watching my fellows' faces crack with fear.
I'd found a separate secret in the dream of death;
dubious contentment in the dead eye of being.

"But O, how quickly I slipped the still center of that being!
For, sunk to the murkiest floor of sleep, I dreamed
my cold companions now revealed to me the death

they called the dead man's second going: his
                                   death in the heart
of the living. And then in a vision of purest fear
I saw all who knew me changed to corpses.

"I saw that the earth was a sack of corpses;
saw them swollen, putrid, ugly in their being,
saw myself there too, tasted gall, smelled my fear,
saw all who would forget me die the double
                                   death I dreamed,
and faithful friends too, saw dead; dead in the world's heart,
dead in the perfect nullity, dead in this green skull of death.

"The corpses all around me vanished while I dreamed
and I woke to the watery world of fear, my trembling heart
and whole being drenched by the rising flood of death."

IV

These various baths, banquets,
dances *are* hereditary.
Everyone but you seems
appropriately dressed.
The butler who announces you
to the ashen habituees

of these vast apartments
cries, "M. Pelops!" stammers,
grows confused, gurgles
when he clears his throat—
fails to recognize your name.
It appears you are not expected

yet; that, once again,
you have arrived in advance
of a proper invitation.
A certain serrated mirth
suggests an explanation:

Is it that you have been deceived?

V

With sickened, crusted eyes we searched the curve
of the long swells for least ruffle of the slow
slick wave heave the days that followed
our stormy fratricide while the wind sat still
and distant as judgment on our burning
needs and the sun hung high over us

and the sea became a glassy tort reducing us
to beastliness, tongue swoll to the palate's curve,
mind dwindling with the body's burning
under the fiery wheel that ground us fine and slow
against the stone of the flat sea. All was still
except the fins of the sharks that followed

patiently waiting as if they had always followed,
unwavering in their bellies' suave knowledge of us,
always there when one grew finally still,
as if they could plot our fall along some insensate curve,
calculating the fatal drift, the slow
decline against the fixed violence of the sun's burning.

And now memory of the sacrifice of many sat burning
in our heads like suns, our thoughts now followed
by a gutted, bloody torso twisting in slow
mimes of fishes; a vision that will never leave us,
fastened to our sleep's uneasy curve
as we were fastened to the surface of the still

waters. The ocean and our thoughts were fetid and still
and memory and the sun were ever burning,
turn and turn about to the day's curve
while the shifting ciphers of sea and sky were followed
like a vague riddle of vital consequence to us.
But all the answer we ever got was the globe's slow

rotation into the chilling dark and the sun's slow
lift of its insupportable light overhead and the still
vision of the woman's open body that never left us.
Caught there in the beastliest pull of burning,
at last submitting to our fate, we followed
the bleak sequence of our situation's curve,

the path of the curve as certain as it was slow,
inescapable as the still sea and the sun's burning:
No shark ate the next of us to fall, and all who followed.

VI

From up there in the bright
and insubstantial air
your foreign ways filter down
to those for whom you may be
the god made manifest;
that is to say, available.

It is a proposition you
might wish to study, for
behind the ripple of surface glaze
their movements describe the mystery
of a certain dance for you
who are so alien, so sweet.

These are the eaters of boots
and bottles and expectations;
your body's anxious bachelors;
creatures of muscular compulsions.
(When you finally arrive,
their eyes will eat you up.)

VII

So much has followed to confirm the horror of that raft,
why should its ramshackle of dying still clamor at us.
Desperate, we ourselves would eat the flesh of corpses.
Well we know the secret shudder in the pitch
of the great pivot, the fear the burning
sun shows the other side of night.
This world has rolled past many a horrible death
and never been known to slow,
change curve, alter any article of being
on account of the human heart.
Why should this particular memory then disturb our sleep?
Does it remind you of some fearful thing you dreamed?

Of such calamities are made the dreams all have dreamed.
In the sleep of each of us a similar memory,
call it specific, is the reef that wrecks the heart.
And the graph of all being plots the same curve,
though the plotting may be slow.
Fear of death, varied only in detail, has rolled
over us like waves since the first mind in the night
anticipated the day's burning. This knowing begat fear,
and ever after the inward ear was tuned to the pitch
of the calling corpses. As we, Reader, tune it still.
O the futility of such vigilance in us:
So fragile this raft of words—this flesh, how avidly followed.

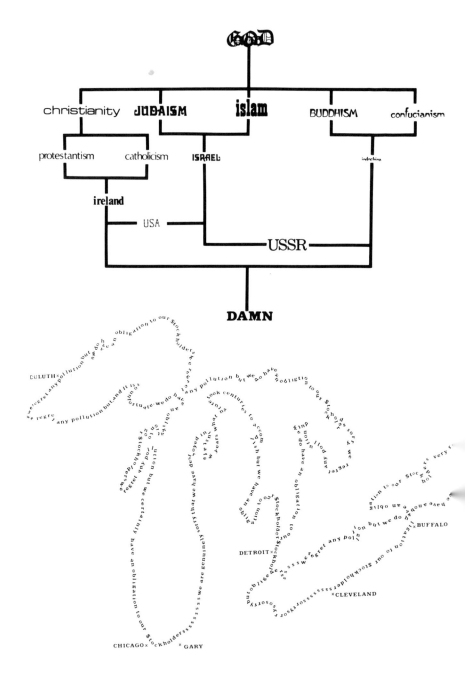

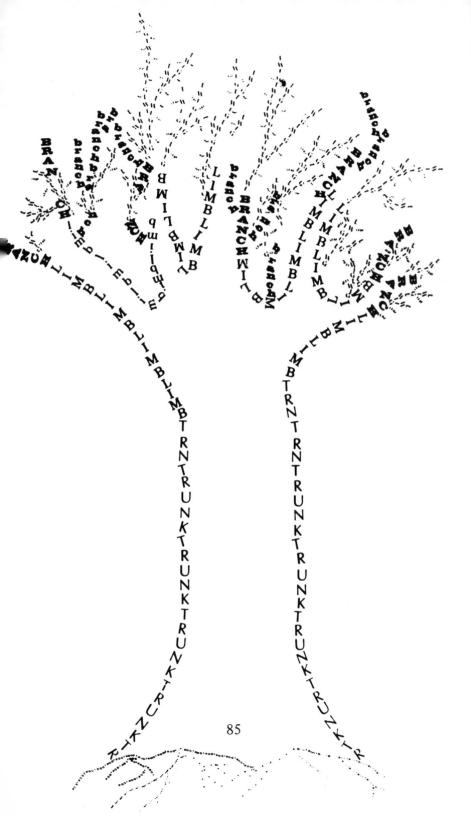

85

ROBERT HAHN

Words From the Housewife

The milkman's broken bottles are just
not enough, they're almost blunt
and I get so lonesome for the print
of your boot

Will you push the scrabble-squares up my ass
and pull them out again one by one
as I come? I understand
this is done in Turkey with a chain of beads
but yours is the only
language I love

It's just not enough
to scream about the patriarchy all day long, no
I need you
in your pullman-porter's uniform
hammering on me to the click of the keys

I put the kids
in the freezer, they'll keep: turn on
the lights and leave
the blinds up
I want to show the world you're mine

And you were afraid I wouldn't be faithful!
Will you burn your books
if I swear
to eat the flame?

To the Stolen Children

Remember there is someone who loves you terribly
Someone who wants to take you away

The man will say
I've come to take you home/but he doesn't
Later he says *I am your father*
what can you believe?
You will see Niagara Falls and the Grand Canyon

Your mother seeks out magicians
Her spells and curses roam the earth
but no one ever comes to the door

The woman will scream: Get in the car
you'll have a new home/but you don't
Your father goes to court
When he arrives, the door is open
the cupboard is empty
the oven cold

Of course it may be different

You return to your father, hands full of coins
and precious stones, the wicked woman dead

You are freed from the monster and restored
to your mother who has never ceased to pray

But remember what I've said
Press your ear to the wall when they talk at night
when the man grows dark, the woman wild
They are hopeless and baffled
You will never understand them

Of course, they may be laying plans
for your survival: you will grow up, unmolested

rest by the fire and rock your children
and sing this song: There are no wolves
We love you the only way we know

They will wake full-grown in the moonlit wood
starting at shadows
thinking Who is the thief

Interrogation

When they take us into our
separate rooms with one-way windows, what
will you say? I'll spill my guts

about the time you took the liquor
& books and left me by the lake it was
your idea to visit/you'll tell them

all about my silences, the tawdry
motives of my finest hours, staunch
stands I took when I couldn't think of

anything else...I'll tell them you were
behind it all! how long I protected
your weakness but no more! She

pretended to have opinions that were
only reactions, see? got your person
red-handed, the smoking pistol, pals

She said it didn't matter but she
had it figured out to the last detail
waiting like a cat for my mistake

She planned the whole job, the Brinks
take the daylight Tiffany snatch United
hijack, she's a master-mind gentlemen I'll

tell you whatever you want, write it
up & throw us down in the same dark
hole, we need some time together

Getting Through the Fifties:
The Starkweather Case Revisited

"Just keep quiet and we're not going to hurt you"

"Lie down over there and close your eyes"

So that was the Fifties
That was one way
to get through them

somnolent, insomniac, in the dazed colleges
making up the news: a 19-year-old
no less moronic or more aware
of what he meant
than Billy the Kid

but we gave him a motive, a nimbus of despair
a James Dean look

planted him out there in the deadly heartland
neither college-material nor an athlete

and he went, the way we wanted
laying down rubber

gunning down his girlfriend's mother
a steel-works president
a salesman from Great Falls, Montana
and seven others

going through the roadblock
between a hundred and a hundred and ten

all of his victims innocent bystanders

nursing our beers
after the library closed at 11:00

That was one way
to get through the evening

A Bad Dream in the Commune

The women are ranged on one side of the loft
They don't like the men, their *macho* trips, locked
into roles, indecisive and demanding
respect, leaning on words

Still (I observe) a basis for the
Good Life resides with these folks
who agree on their politics, and if some insist
that jealousy's innate while others claim
any number can play

I say, who knows? which makes me in
theory an ideal communard
In practice they take me for a journalist

who must go back, slick story in hand, to
lousy martinis limping toward divorce

The men are out kicking clods with their boots
They despise the women, their rootless anger, awash
in ambiguity, obsessed with roles, ransacking
muddled rhetorics

When the men return, the two camps cook meals
Because the food is identical, they
eat it together, in a circle, at peace
Later they smoke and look out at the mountains

forgetting me entirely listen I'm
hungry! o.k. you're right it's a bumper-
sticker life honk
if you're horny honk for impeachment if you

love the Lord if you're bored, if
you hate me you're lying you're a
honky honk if you're dying (sweet
Jesus the geese
are flying and little's laid in
for the winter: wake up, what's your plan?
We must change our lives)

BRIAN SWANN

An Education in Tongues

There is much to be said
on both sides
It is not important
how one gets there
The fact is the tracks lie
over and above all considerations
of destination

Do nights all have different colors
though they are the same nights?
The food taste limps or exults
at the touch of a word?
One can hardly believe that
though the country native to the word
both approaches and recedes
as mystery opens in the direction
of understanding and closes
in the direction of understood

The full are fed what they impart
The intelligence of everyone reaches
even to beggar-children
and the shop-shelves are stocked
with words whose full flavor
you will never know and which
you might prefer to stay that way
as you bring ordinary technology to bear
on the exploration of the contents

The ignorant perhaps
keep the alternate colors
clear in their clumsy moist touch

Somewhere in between perhaps is a land
where everything behaves just as one knows
it ought not yet logically
Insects for example head into
a full moon obeying light
and darkening it with their wingbeats

Dreams are always in the original
and here the person of tongues
resolves into one language
where all intelligence fades to aboriginal
and years of discipline are undone
in one night

It is in this land
the ignorant and half-
educated walk with their eyes open
deliberately refusing to open
more than a slit
Here daily needs are amazing
and what one reads has the force of oracle
No large claims are made but everything is met
and conquers by being un-conquered
The light of the intellect is out
insects swarm into the moon
and make it gold make themselves
golden golden as honey in the
aftermath of words

This is the dream of the intellect forfended
the intellect defended against itself
To stay here
is to stay caught between
unhappiness and voluptuousness
One cannot devote more than a lifetime to it
There is also the study of languages

Vita Silenziosa

day is found
when it shines
through the whole bone
and the light that runs up the cliff
from the sea-gardens
brushes against hedges
and hangs in tufts
a signal it is time
for the swine to be maddened
and pitch down

*

there is the lamp and there is the chair
and the candle is at the dark mirror's side
its glow makes faces
on a gold mask

a figure in brown running
always the same size
running in the confines of the place
that stretches through the room
through the door
through the night that has only now
arisen and booms like a bronze gong
sails its plates into the air
quietly
quiet as a dog by an old master
quiet as an eyelash
quiet as the bread I hold in my hands
a smiling mouth
a mind closed
close as the nightingale
bubbling in the gold broom
under the open window

*

in this eye a beam balances
in this hand a blade rusts
from this tongue a coat is taken
on this tongue a night shines through
on this head glass keeps all distances
on these feet dust is deserted

Capricho

The cat watches with me
Yawning and ears pricked at the corner

Goya sits deaf and syphilitic
He has done the last of his *caprichos*—

Capricci—Piranesi's word for his
"Imaginary Prisons" of Rome past

Both sit smoking in the Home of the Deaf Man
They too see something in the corner

Goya stretches and strokes the cat
He walks straight into Saturn's gob

The living-room is quiet
Piranesi looks about him and

Pulls huge keys from his pocket
He opens a cell and lies down on the wet concrete

The cat pounces and tears the corner to shreds

WILLIAM SPRUNT

On the Run

Ritual for extracting pain
Feet chasing themselves
Through acres of cow's breath
Across the bones of an afternoon.

Solitary rite
Like digging a grave
Room for just one
Digger or dead.

Mud

A mixture, always
Nothing pure
Particles of day, night
Bone, hair, dreams
Refuse for the collector
Who has no place to put it.

*

The writing appeared
Near the end of a dry season
But I cannot read it.
Perhaps I need a new mirror.

*

Father Hippocrates
I have a strange disorder
I have no heart.
    "We have a remedy

For that illusion.
Cover yourself with damp earth.
It dries first
Where the warmth is.
Dig there."

Exercise in Solitude

If I take silence by the ears
will it crumble to the will
teach it to heel and obey
pretend I cut the cords
not for ordinance sake
to hear the heart beat?

I have seen the night in mouths
open between question and answer
looked for proof
the ghost of the mirror
where a message might appear
but never has.

There is one more fear:
the sound of an empty room.

Leave the banquet table set
feast on linear conversations
celebrate the lack of faces
toast the kinship of the dumb
use the hand that moves the pen
to brush the shivered night aside.

CAROL FROST

The Salt Lesson

Looking inside the bony plate, perceive
the gray sponge matter that from its depth
breeds without moving.
Colors belong to the surface, reckon
with the wind mounting tidal waves,
clouds' cover, or a ripple of sun.

Underneath, the seeping calculation,
the dark crevasses and only spots of artificial
light. What the mind allows, sucks
without bloat. Unearthly life,
a grouper eats a man whole, the gold
doubloons; something precious,

spontaneous. The gull returns to the sea
food broken down by sharks.
The mind is a sullen scavenger
with the belly and bowels of a god.

Water city, this impure taker
returns so little, a bubble of stupidity,
a salt piece of itself, of what it endures.

Night Is No More Or Less Important
Than Bad Circles Or "Ksing."

for Richard Hugo

Sick stomach. Bix Beiderbecke
rolling and keeping his horn like a small boat
on the swell of jazz. I'm trying to read poetry
to fall asleep. Flies
dropping like pelicans in the bed.

98

I brush them, sick, away
who live in the windows and lose them at night.
They fly bad circles.

My husband's sock, a drooping pet
with its otter smell, clings
though I have thrown it off the bed.
My son starts a song with remarkable swing
about cereal and birds—the feeder we hung today.
He chortled at eating a bird's wing at lunch.
Everything is equal for food
and poetry. "Ksing," closing down
of the cymbal. High hat.

Who would eat flies? Words?
Bits of used wax paper, wings or fish scales on the bed,
small black ovals, their heads, little gritty orchids,
these flies broken up in the storm and noise
of my thrashing to sleep. Bird hieroglyphics
and a fuzz of parts float like cream in the air.
The rhythm of song and horn rocking the night
takes me around, "ksing," around
in the whirlpool of recognized things.

PERRY OLDHAM

Local Destruction

Steam had mustered since we'd heard
that we might be moved out.
Then it was official   we transferred
into a raw new hootch.
So we threw a demolition party
when we left.
Ripped down thin partitions that we'd built
and painted   kicked them into chunks
upended metal lockers   threw ticking
mattresses in corner heap
tossed confetti made of letters magazines
western novels outdated *Stars and Stripes*
dismantled the screened-in porch (no room for one
at the new hootch) piece by piece
slashed the screens and plastic sheets
lobbed the two-by-fours like javelins inside
the hootch then bammed them into scraps
sprayed shaving cream on walls
shattered old Jim Beam and Smirnoff
bottles on the floor   aimed our empty
beer and soda cans at dusty
ceiling lights   when the last was out
we filled a tub with water and flushed it onto the floor.
The fucking Army put us in this hootch
and we worked to fix it up
now they give it to another outfit.
Let them make their own improvements.

Hygiene

Watch who you fuck with
and wear a rubber

They're cheap. You get them in the
BX

Wash up when you're through
with soap and water

Hot as you can stand it. Chances
are, the women

You meet downtown the hootch
maids on the

Compound, chances are
they've got

VD or TB
or both. Now we

Can cure most of what you bring
in but listen

Up. There's a disease here
Black Syph

You catch that there's not much
we can do

For you. And forget about
going home

A man from this same outfit
served his three-

Hundred and sixty-five days, and
Black Syph

Showed up in his last urine
test. You

Guessed it. He didn't go
home. Sorry

About that. They don't want
that bug

Back in the world. Watch out
for steambaths

You think you can have some fun
downtown

No sweat. Think again
Some girl

Downtown giving head
in a steambath gave

The clap to fifteen GIs last
month, fif-

Teen! before we tracked her down
One last

Thing. Don't be like the GI
hadn't seen

His wife for eight months. Went
on R&R

Gave VD to his wife and
she got pregnant

Men that baby was born blind and
without a nose

Think about it. Maybe he
could have prevented

The whole thing if he'd just
worn a rubber.

Saigon Tea

Fatigued, Lily finishes a cigarette,
leans back against the wall. Across the room Mai
            warms a soldier's lap, her arms around
        his neck. Xuan plays tic tac toe, laughs with her

GI. But Lily wants to chat, sip her tea,
rest for a while. She is getting old. At her
            age, most bargirls are working in
        bath-houses. Are dead. Married. Mama-sans

in bars of their own. Yet the soldiers still find
her appealing, tight under clinging pants and
            blouse, wearing little make-up. She came
        south from Hanoi in 1954,

after Dien Bien Phu and the two Vietnams,
has worked many bars, known many soldiers. Life
            could have been worse: she's had pretty clothes,
        food, liquor, money for doctors. But she's

getting old. She will open a bar for the
troops, if she can save enough. Or she'll go to
            Marseilles. Her husband is in Marseilles
        since 1958, is in trade in

Marseilles. She will go there to live with him, meet
him on the docks, speak French that she learned from the
            troops in Hanoi. Be a merchant's wife
        in Marseilles, cook rice in many pots.

PETER KLAPPERT

The Spider, Unsurprised

Four months content
to mend the depredations
of the wind, while the great sphere
became a small sphere
and I, wound out, inside
cataleptic, six legs
on the graph of my season,
sensed your flurried wings
and registered a gradual
descent.
                 My poor
assassin, you seem inclined
to thwang this net again,
the last wasp of summer's
last encore: should I
in my conceit deny
the itch of instinct, feign
sleep, or we, lovers
of a lesser order, dance
the sad ballet once more?

The Trapper

I am digging a pit
deeper than I will need.

Already
on the other side of this mountain
something is crying in a small hoarse voice.

It is breaking its teeth on my teeth.

Some shy animal is taking its paw
apart in the darkness.
Some poor animal is looking through its bones.

When I grab at my lungs they contract
like an old leather bellows.

Something the size of a very small boy
is kicking against that trap.

Gun, White Castle

All I need is a regular
cup of coffee. I am not suicidal.
I have a gun.
                    An Iver Johnson
.32 snub. It cost me sixty-three dollars
but that doesn't mean I'll use it.

You know. The lights in this place
are too white. A gun
is heavy and
                    thick like a black fish.
I can conceal it in my coat, in my car,
I can stand it up in a medicine chest.

I know all the arguments. A gun is specific.
Those who are not effective—you learn
to use real dynamite.
                    A small gun
no more than twenty
or twenty-four ounces. You keep it oiled.
That's not suicidal.

I left it at home on the night stand.
I saw it in a magazine. Everyone
needs a gun. To keep his

thoughts honest. You can file your
nails on the handle.
                        When I finish up
here, I will learn how to use it.

          R. S. V. P.
                              −there will be plenty of regrets

      When the exhibition opens, it's
someone you've always
wanted to know, and his smile
is wider than your own bewildered mouth.

              "Whose face is this?"
you whisper, as he turns
from poet to matron, from harpsichordist
to priest. But the gallery walls
dissolve in water-lights.

He is a paragon of mirrors:
transposed into your portraits, you
and the staring others
fail to note the prisms of his personality
or that
          gazing straight into him
you see the people at your left and right.

Oh, he brings to the room
a bright focus
              but under the flasks of his eyes
splashes cold water.

              He has no shadow
or we are
all his shadow, and loving
everything you see
does not mean you love yourself.

MICHAEL WATERS

Leaves & Ashes
for Michael Ryan

1

Sometimes,
when the bars close,
the streets seem to whisper in rain
like women mistaken for mother.

Her skin waves on a clothesline.
Her crotch bleeds over Chinatown.
The three graces of city life
moon in a doorway:

One is called *spare change.*
One is named *fire-in-the-trashcan.*
One resembles *death on a menu.*

Maybe the dark one
hauls you to her breast
like a blind lover on wedding night.

You would like to disappear.
You imagine dawn
opening your heart like a room.
Anyone could live there.

2

A thief can carry sorrow in his arms
like a daughter
almost saved from drowning.

An uncle can be silent for years.
You can wrestle your heart
at the nearest bar for a drink.

Suppose the memories hang on you
like a large coat,
an animal hugging your back.

How can you tell her to let go?
When you close your eyes
you imagine a winter sun
burning through mist,

or a young girl who wakes
to feel her breasts for the first time,
that look of surprise on her face,
like the magician
who discovers a strange bird in his coat.

Wedding Poem

There have been days
when I felt my larger self
hovering around me,
an awkward angel.
We both enter you,
a spirit of flesh.

I don't mean to be
contradictory.
This is simpler:
one night, when I was drunk
and dirty from loving
another man's wife,
you took me, gently,
and washed my small bones like rice.

Leaving America

Gulls wash a dune of stone,
weather-beaten & hollow,
the shape of an Indian's skull
seen clear across the water.

None of us has eaten for years.
The country drifts in the Pacific
and the landscape sways with dream.
Scavengers arrive like lice.

On the tracks an abandoned boxcar,
a few loose ties covered with weed,
something like a family.
So many forgotten lives to settle,

products of the California boom.
One railroad spike dangerous as gold
flashes violence on the horizon,
a razor tucked like money in a shoe.

There is still another country,
less romantic, where three men
who dragged a girl from her car
are killed on the tracks near Fresno.

Maybe a crazy brother, maybe a spike
in the brain, maybe, like Thoreau,
a railroad through the lungs
to carry a circus of loving geeks.

Feathers whirl in my ribcage too,
delicate birds leaving America.
I haven't the stomach for it.
A porcupine in love with himself

stands a better chance,
stumbling across this dark lawn.

Water breaks like history on the republic.
I am so full of good wishes and goodbyes.

The Dead

Maybe the dead are asleep,
it is certainly hard enough work.
I wake as if from winter,
a rosary of perspiration
staining my thin white lips.

On the farm nothing is easy.
All night I strain the tractor
to pull the stump into light.
So much is rotten here:
the sad green odor of mushrooms
like a stale air in the room.

Maybe this continues for life.

One morning the darkness
seems to root
somewhere in my legs,
and I leave the soul
in its warm bed of moss
and drive to the tree.

Nothing:
a few ducks taking water,
trailing their young,
like women who laugh at me.

So I imagine
the tree is not gone,
that young girls sunbathe
in its loving shade
on rising blankets of bread.

Who wouldn't give a picnic
to be enveloped in fog?

When the air
seems to press its skull
as a wafer on my face,
when the sky seems that close...

I think of it this way:

a tree is nothing
so much
as a belief in sleep,
in whatever rises from darkness.

Night Fishing

There is a fish so large
the sky can't hold it,
these arms open wide
but the fish swims away...

and there is a land,
no bullshit,
where we can be happy
and hug our fathers, once,
before they die.

PETER MEINKE

Chicken Unlimited

Today is our 16th anniversary
the suet anniversary, everything
turning to fat
At my side as I drive squats Chicken Unlimited
the 16-piece box: we have 4 kids
sometimes I think we eat too much chicken
it makes us want to kill each other

Our house is surrounded by oaks, azaleas
thriving on 6-6-6 and chicken bones
Chicken Unlimited is afraid of being alone, is
beautiful:
"Scarlet circles ring your eyes
your bill as black as jet
like burnished gold your feathers gleam
your comb is devil-red"
I think the sky is falling

Chicken Unlimited constantly breaks his neck
against an invisible shield
he can't get at the flowers

He is ambitious: wants to be president
wants to fuck the Queen
he wants to be Johnny Carson
he takes extension courses at night
but doesn't know what to think

I'm stuck in the traffic on 12th street
the man behind is honking like a crazed goose
I think he's after Chicken Unlimited

My son comes home bloody
"If I run, they call me chicken,

if I fight, he beats the shit out of me"
That's right, I say
that's the way it goes

Chicken Unlimited is jumping on my chest
its beak rakes my face
I think it wants to kiss me
I think it wants to eat me alive

I say, Chicken Unlimited
your kisses taste like wine
but I'm too old for this sort of thing.

In the sky the constellations realign
the Big Dipper points to Chicken Unlimited
the rings of Saturn are grain
for its celestial gizzard
the sky is surely falling

One of my dreams is playing centerfield
in Yankee Stadium: C.U. is at bat,
smashes a towering drive I race back back
over the artificial grass
but the ball becomes an egg becomes
a bomb
as I/we crash together at the monument

Chicken Unlimited worries about his input
he wants to make it perfectly clear
but it still comes out cluckcluck
cluck cluck
he is weak on his relative pronouns

Daughter (age 9): Where do babies come from?
Mother: Why, from inside a woman.
D.: Yeah, how'd they get in there?
M.: Well, let's see, how to explain it...
D.: Yeah, the old chicken in the bun, right?

Right.

Chicken Unlimited has such energy!
Like our kids
chicken tracks in the sooty snow.
Still stuck in this insane traffic
man behind still honking me deaf
wanting to get home to my wife, my children
this crazy urge to stick my head
out the window, and yell
Compliments to the Chef!

Everything We Do

Everything we do is for our first loves
whom we have lost irrevocably
who have married insurance salesmen
and moved to Topeka
and never think of us at all.

We fly planes & design buildings
and write poems
that all say Sally I love you
I'll never love anyone else
Why didn't you know I was going to be a poet?

The walks to school, the kisses in the snow
gather, as we dream backwards, sweetness with age:
our legs are young again, our voices
strong and happy, we're not afraid.
We don't know enough to be afraid.

And now
we hold (hidden, hopeless) the hope
that some day
she may fly in our plane
enter our building read our poem

And that night, deep in her dream,
Sally, far in darkness, in Topeka,
with the salesman lying beside her,
will cry out
our unfamiliar name.

DANIELA GIOSEFFI

Some Slippery Afternoon

A silver watch you've worn for years
is suddenly gone
leaving a pale white stripe
blazing on your wrist.

A calendar marked with
all the appointments you meant to keep
disappears
leaving a faded spot on the wall
where it hung.
You search the house, yard, trash cans for weeks
and never find it.

One night the glass in your windows
vanishes
leaving you sitting in a gust of wind.

You think how a leg is suddenly lost
beneath a subway train
or a taxi wheel
some slippery afternoon.

The child you've raised for years
combing each lock,
tailoring each smile, each tear,
each valuable thought,
suddenly changes to a harlequin,
joins the circus passing in the street
never to be seen again.

One morning you wash your face,
look into the mirror,
find the water has eroded your features,

worn them smooth as a rock in a brook.
A blank oval peers back at you
too mouthless to cry out.

Through the Eye of the Needle

Death is a country where people wonder
and worry what it is like to live.
The sullen wish to live and live soon,
to be done with death.
The happy want to stay dead forever
wondering
will it hurt to live
and is there death after death

Eggs
—for Francis Ponge

Eggs that come from chickens,
squeezing oblong from their feathered bottoms.
Tapered ovals opaque with white
filled with albumen. Delicate thickness!
I've eaten them raw, sucking them from a pin-hole
carefully made in the shell.
I've pressed my lips to the hole and sucked
until the white carried the yolk out in one mass
                              onto my tongue.
I've beaten them and butter-fried them into
                              spongy yellow chunks.
I've left their sunny sides up until the whites
                    were glazed like plastic,
and then, pricked the orange yolk with the sharp
                              point of a fork
and watched it slowly spread and ooze over the plate.

117

Then, I've sopped it up with toast
until the toast was soggy and limp
and dripped when lifted to the mouth.
I've boiled them and listened
to the click of shells
as they wobbled in the bubbling water.
Small sounds of thunder. Shell against metal.
Then I've cracked them and peeled them,
pulling the residue of skin-like membrane from them,
then sliced or bit into the their shine of rubbery white
with yellow paste center.
I've lathered them into my hair with shampoo.
I've mixed them with cheeses and mushrooms and onions.
Today I've bought one hundred dozen of them—
farm-fresh, Grade A., large white eggs in spongy grey
cardboard cartons.
I've arranged them around the bathroom, their
                                        cartons opened,
exposing rows of gleaming white lumps.
One thousand two hundred of them.
Delicate shells threaten to burst and spray yolk over tile.
I choose the first and tap it lightly on the porcelain tub.
A thin line shatters the cool shell.
I violate the crack, thumb-nail first,
and slowly separate the shell, tearing the inside membrane
with a small sound of skin
and plop it into the tub.
Its nucleus of yellow pops as it lands on the hard
                                        surface below.
Slowly from the ragged half-shell
a clear string of mucus, a long thin globule, follows after it.
I take the next and the next,
crack each on the tub edge and plop it to the hard surface,
watching the yellow yolks break, ooze, and splatter.
I keep on with my work until the tub fills enough
                                        for me to watch
the yolks bounce into the thick liquid,
sink a little, then buoy to the surface.

When I drop, at last, the one-thousand-two-hundredth,
the tub is full, and the mucoid surface is cobbled with yolks.
Slowly I put one bare leg into the tub, letting
                              the viscous mass
rise up my body as I slide down in up to my chin.
I lie perfectly still, listening to the silent squish
of the mass that surrounds me.
I take some of the fluid and smear it into my hair
and over my skin.
I move and thrash my arms and legs about until
                              the mixture of
yolk and white is thoroughly blended.

DAVID PERKINS

Growing Up

how we went around in a
daze
how we were hypnotized by the sound
of baseball bats
and the sighing of nylon thighs
how we were struck dumb
by the incredible pink of chewing
gum
how we walked around disguised as
one another
how we lay awake at night watching
the dark breeze
flow over our bodies
and were so keen for touch we lived
a quarter inch above our own skins

how we woke up falling
falling back into ourselves like snow
falling on our warm arms
how we changed to water and now
rise and fall inside ourselves like
a tide pulled
by an everyday moon
how we get so high, and no higher

Doctor, I Dream of Sleep

Doctor, I don't know if I've got the right
attitude.
I come out of my apartment every morning
with my hands up.
I feel my life melting away like a lifesaver

on my own tongue.
I used to be on top of it, doctor.
I could tell the year and model of a car
just by feeling the door handle.
Now my mind is going.
Thoughts occur in me as if my brain were a lake
some kid was skipping rocks over.
Meanwhile, the past obsesses me.
I can't count to ten without feeling like an
historical figure.
It's not fair,
doctor. I used to talk to God.

I dream of being a lion, doctor.
I want to sleep in the sun for eighteen hours
without feeling guilty about it,
and then wander down to the river
to chew on a few antelope.
I want to have some cubs running around.
Don't tell me it's not possible. Don't tell me
it's too late.

But tell me about the cattle tick that sits
for seventeen years on a blade of grass,
waiting for something warm and moving to trigger
its life.
Tell me it's all heavy inside me like bullets
in a revolver.
Tell me how even now Africa is hurrying toward the sun
for the first time in its life.
Tell me what a good day it will be for sleeping.

And tell me how the soft brown cubs no bigger
than my paws
will climb over me while I sleep,
sure and fond of me as if I were a rock
with a name.

LAURANCE WIEDER

The Paradise Rug

When we woke up at 7:30, it snowed
Last night. I thought the bedroom
Preternaturally warm at 3:00 A.M.
And it was: snow's the proof. You left
For work at the music factory, saying
"Meet me at the church at 12:10 for Purcell"
And locked the door. I dreamed of snowy parks
And haircuts through mid-morning, as the snow turned
From paper plates to urban glop. Last night
I read you *L'Allegro* and *Il Penseroso*
And you fell asleep, but I didn't mind
Because I left the storied towers of Manhatto
For a time, and entered the pure feeling
World, where feeling is thought, and shade
The color of windows from the street at sunset
Grows, quiet, happy. I could bless the known
Stars and the houseplants freshly sprayed, then,
My days stretched like an archipelago, and large
And small, or neatly pressed between the leaves.
But back. You wore a green coat in the pew
As I blew in at the homily, a cloud.
They knelt. We kissed. Two Purcell anthems,
A prayer for management and labor in hard times,
Then to a counter for a cup of coffee. You were sorry
To bring me out into the weather, but I didn't mind
Because it took me once again
Into the mysterium tremendum, and to you.
Don't wake up cold in the middle of the night.
I've paid the rent and pilloried the landlord.
As a child, nobody would play with me.
I left the playground tired and alone.
I didn't cry, but swore
When I grew up my life would pale
Their neglect, would grow more true

Than mockery or envy. In the center of my room
Is a Paradise rug, and everything but poetry
Is like sex between small children, of no use
To them or us, save as a pastime. Four o'clock.
The key in the lock. The chains untwisting.

A Letter to His Sister

It was hard for you to put up with your older brother
Who doesn't ask properly for permission to arrive,
Who arrives under his own clouds, and who sleeps,
Almost sick, in the living room just when the sun
Is best, in afternoon. You are right to bridle
At my intrusion. But I wonder what you're doing.
The new puppy has a sweet disposition, but you
Make no attempt to housebreak her, and I am afraid
She will settle into bad habits. Don't you see
The kitchen shouldn't be a kennel? You tell yourself
"Not now. I will be gone for weeks, and when I come back
Then she will be trained." Meanwhile, a bad smell
Lingers in the kitchen, and time is passing.
I wonder if you see your own ideas, as I see
I am awkward. I don't want you to get angry with me,
But feel you would be mistaken to put off training
Your young dog, who grows faster than you or I,
And soon must be something more than sweet.

PATRICIA GOEDICKE

Where We Are Going

Where we are going the sky clears
Wider and bluer than heaven but not present, not present
To our breaking ears

Though the sweat of our bodies sweetens
And the odor of our genitals is like dried apples

Where we are going our joints cry out
Every morning in a different voice,

Friends vanish,in the cold
Where we are going our arms
Gradually empty themselves to the wind,

Where we are going our footsteps disappear
Shrouded in foghorns, in fingers smothering
The brittle moss of our veins

Where we are going, on the path
To a cobwebbed attic, a dissolving
Far ahead of us like a fisherman's net

Like a foreign tongue, like a piece of bread
We are eaten, we are full of holes.

At Every Major Airport

Dear Passengers, I hate to sound reactionary about this,
But even if you believe you really *are* in His hands,
Even if you are able to pray like my husband
(Who also takes sleeping tablets, and drinks)

There's no getting around it, unfortunately
I think you had better be ready to die
When you fly.

The sheer terror of it has been written about often
In poetry, in prose—
Even therapy groups have been formed to combat this fear

But it can't be helped,
Always
At every major airport in the world

First you have to crawl through a caterpillar
Lugging your hand luggage up its guts,
Next through an open gate, a scream
Exhaust tearing at your hair

And then you're in for it:
Thumb closes the door

And you, poor miniature you
Whether you smile nervously at the tiny stewardess
Or cling to the soft pad of the palm

By God you better know it:
That old belly of an earth mother just rolled over,
Stuck up a couple of hands
And caught you, just like that.

Right back in the old coffin, uterus, ice box
There you go again;

Driving an automobile it's easy to get out
Whenever you want to, even a bus or a train stops
Once in awhile, at country crossings

But not here, thousands of miles high,

Nobody stops here,
Even He doesn't stop here
Or, if He does
His intentions are by no means absolutely clear—

Better just lean forward and use the vomit bag
And remember you have nothing to fear but the man

Who, after all, invented this whole business but which one?
The one with the pistol that looks like a Didee doll
The kind that can pee blood all over the whole cabin

Or the one who, after inventing this next-to-
                              impossible machine
Of course finds it hard to believe in a God about Whom
However, there have been several well documented reports:

How, over Lake Pontchartrain, in Louisiana, the
                              pilot said he felt
"as if a huge Hand suddenly grabbed the ship and
                              tossed it up in the
and then let go"

whereupon the pilot regained control but there are
                              other incidents,
squawks over the recording device,
"it's as if. . . . . .someone's . . . . got hold of us. . . .
Then silence, then the scream of the wind
Picked up after the crash.

Success Story

1. When he was a young man, an invalid
    his father the doctor said No Hope.

2. Stuck in a blood box he vomited up failure

126

3. But having been born among dangerous men
   by women, his enemies

4. He spat on his four sisters

5. He stood up and limped

6. On their shoulders he went to Medical School

7. Where he mastered the mind, became

8. Expert in illusion, drove

9. Everything real before him,

10. And some of his patients loved him
    and some not:

11. Gunning his motorcycle nose he roared
    over their bent backs as if they were his mother's

12. For the pain never ended,
    finally he married

13. A mistake, of course, a woman

14. Weaker than himself, he said

15. To his three timid daughters
    Climb me you will fall,

16. Speak to me of your mother you will break your backs

17. For my women are my puppets,
    rags I use to tie up my wounds,

18. For my women are for lying down on

19. For you know I did not deliberately make
                                    of your deaf

127

now dead mother a doormat:

20.   She should have lived long after me but I survived.

The Dog Who Comes From Nowhere

Pressed between the flat sides of the buildings
Like a button under a steam iron she's tough,
Absorbed in her own thoughts

She strolls down the street
Under the noon sun but she's not hot,
There's a humming in her head

That is pure efficiency, she thinks
At last she's arrived, after all the dirty tricks

Who cares about the wrinkles,
The loose threads on her dress?

The buildings are beginning to lean
Together, over her head

But she refuses to notice, like a wooden doll
With straw-colored, graying hair

She pulls on her Camel and strides along,
She hardly even notices the dog

Who comes from nowhere,
Who does not even live on her street

Until he is upon her,
He walks by like a stranger and then turns

Suddenly he takes a chunk out of the scrawny hand
Whose calluses swell up, whose liver spots spread

Faster and faster because this is Mexico,
The only place in the world she *could* come to,

Having buried her heart in Colorado
Along with her husband and no money
On top of everything now this:

The painful series of shots stretching ahead
In accident's mean jaws

The small carton of herself ripped open
The one she wrapped so neatly

Torn apart, shredded
Pieces of paper like sawdust,

Traveler's certificates, licenses
Wedding pictures smashed, scattered, bleeding
All over the main street.

Escalator

Meeting me it was love at first sight:
You named me for my aspirations.

Ascending with me like a serpent's tongue
Into the one heaven of a department store

You called me water flowing uphill
As smooth, as calm

One foot sliding into
The other and that one
Into the next and so

On like a caterpillar unfolding
On bird's feet, precise
Liquid

Jeweled belt going up
Yes truly I am a dream machine
Riding me no one speaks

Electric
Noise bubbles and boils

Like the tubes of a Moog Synthesizer
Yards and yards of me coil
From the basement to the mezzanine

Expanding, contracting, in paradise
Like a zipper silently opening

Up again, down again, smooth
In slow motion hunted

As you, lordly, rise
Without moving hand or foot
Past everything you ever wanted.

After the Second Operation

A little nearer, this time
Fragile as clear glass but singing

It is like being your own target
Balanced on a tightrope, trembling

It is the shape of something
Without shape: joy

Coming and going like heat lightning,
Flashing across the sky.

Leaving the hospital, for awhile
The whole landscape erupts

Into pure ecstasy: cliffs, crags
Sheer drops of delight,
Sudden peaks of pain...

I tell you it is ridiculous
Standing here on one foot

Half the time off balance,
Most of the time blinded
By tears like diamonds in the eyes

But after the long flatness, the plains
And deserts of daily life

It is as if the soul
Were stretching itself, and flying

For now nothing is ordinary: each step
Newness pierces the heart,

The tender horizon of the body tilts
Up one side of the mountain and down the other

For now everything is as it should be, everyday
Danger brandishes its spear
So beautifully, along the way

All around you you can feel it
Glancing off you like the light
That hovers but will not stay.

PETER TRIAS

The Stoneyard

Winter has broken against the bones,
the pieces falling onto the still
chilled fields, the dark winds pounding
into the lean earth, the sinking moon
exploding before me, and now the dead
rising into the moon-ripped night.

I must face these dead who offer me
this terrible love, their easy
weight against me. I am young.
I wander in the graveyard easily.
See there ahead of me! the black angel,
one great wing always lifting.

The Marriage of Here and There

The greyhounds have entered the garden
where, as a child, I saw FDR—
tall ghost before the rose bushes.
That house above the Hudson was mine,
until my godmother went crazy
(confined to an air of cut flowers).
No one recognized me.
Draped black and purple,
ribbons lined the fireplace,
while down the hall
one daughter rose from the analyst's chair
to slip a record on the phonograph.
And, in the museum, a line of children
filed past the family wedding gown,
turning their faces in time
to view my image beyond the door.

Movement in Provence

The butcher loved our French maid,
he strung a wire to the kitchen
and gave us radio. That tiny light
in a Seventeenth Century home, high above
the valley where we found English snobbery
(until I was recognized for my grandmother
moving across the dance floor).
I never dreamed a name could be so valuable.
Hitler would broadcast as *La Bonne* prepared;
and we were speaking French, before the children,
dressed in their pith helmets and white ducks,
clambered up the hillside.
They were my ambassadors, imagine!
Their faces would not sit for a portrait
or the guards at the Italian border where
the bomb turned out to be a disengaged clock.

MICHAEL HOGAN

Letter From My Son

My little boy, no longer small,
writes to me as a stranger writes.
Had all those kitchen miles of crawling
led West, he would be here.
Had I lingered there handcuffed by love,
regret perhaps would not lie thick
as the soap ring in her sink.

Today he writes and wonders
why it was I left and there
is no emotion, no sense
of loss, merely curiosity—
a question a bright child might ask
like: why did biplanes have two wings
and no easy, circular reasoning, please.
The answer, not terribly important to him,
should still be true.

His letter is unanswered and will
perhaps remain so.
We have grown distant
as the sun is from stalactites;
bats flutter blindly in the cold air.
All the wrong questions have been asked
and the correct answers are not true.

A Quiet Orderly Life

The old man's been deadlocked there
in the same basement cell
for six and a half years.
Even the guards can't remember why.

Every day he does two hundred pushups
and runs fifteen miles in place.
He offers himself occasional words of encouragement
and dresses each night in his cleanest blues.
It's a quiet orderly life
and the guard captain says
the old man is content there
and doesn't like to be disturbed.

BART SCHNEIDER

Song for the Woman Singing at the Café Trieste

When you look past
the mandolin player, over

the waitress' straining back
isn't it for me?

Aren't you searching for the brother who drowned
when he was five,

or began, as they told you, climbing
a ladder and never stopped?

I am your brother,
we spent years brooding

in another world.
I am certain we are twins.

Now having lived among Italians
you've learned their strange songs

and how to throw back your neck
wildly to reach the highest notes.

It is clear that it took such abandon
to make this world.

As you sing, everyone in the place
is tilting forward in his chair

yet you're looking for me
past the mandolin player.

TOM HOUSE

Parable of the Sidewalk Tellers

1.

Earbob and the painted carnivores
are dancing on the corner
in five-inch, gleaming platforms,

twirling their pleats,
rearranging their chains,

keeping it as cool
and as in the pants
as possible.

"Ain't no friends in dope,"
whispers Bagboy,

sending children home to nipples,
arms filled with empty bottles.

Papa Jack, teased and tinted,
propped against a sagging door,
sucking on an apple,

adds red eyes to the anguish
of screaming tires, factory whistles,
sirens silent
save to a few.

Bagboy. Quickie in the bathroom.
Tattoos his arm with a ten-penny nail.

Earbob (Tyrannosaurus Peacock)
flexes his veins

in the jungle of a window.

Bubble-top glides by
like an early edition of the ice age;
and, immediately, all dinosaurs
are extinct.

2.

Check-out Girl shoves her groceries
along the conveyor,
smiles (a loving pinch for the vegetables)
offers coupons for her bargains,

wheels her latent basket .
through electric eyes.

Bagboy grins. (The computer balks
where love can't pay.)
Fingers his profits. Rattles
pocket change and skeletons.

Caution lights ring yellow
on the register.
"I'm the new face of love,"
he tells her,

"love under control. I never confuse
lust and greed."

3.

Old Grunt n Groan has retired
from the trade but thrives
in Bagboy's fantasies,

bursting through a shuttered door,

a thick browed, hairy neanderthal,
slamming that cop's head
against the sooty brick

until it was only a wadded trophy,
(worthless on the wall
but priceless on the street)—

One dream chasing another

through stop-and-go people,
bringing a certain delicacy to machines,
debutantes and mustangs,

shrieking at jungle dreams
splattered on their windshields.

4.

Earbob fondles his fantasy.
Melody, the playful whore,
advertises from the marquee.
She is like a cat under his fingers,

arching her back,
purring at his throat.

Bagboy makes change for twenty.
They can wait. They have to.
Standing in the bread line, the
the patient, the meek,
the intermittent.

Everyone sells. That's Bagboy's logic;
the product deals with morals
profit determines the life style.

"How true," agrees Sidewalk
Chairman of the Board,
a rose in his hair
in a neighborhood of pimps,

his surrogate women
squirming in his hips,
smiling to himself
(for he knows what his money buys)

standing at the head
of the withdrawal line,

(the carnivores bitching,
stomping around, starving
as garishly as buzzards)

while Check-Out Girl
makes good her promise,

squeezing sweat from the gold
in his nylon sheath.

                    5.

Climax hits the stands at 4 a.m.
The table of contents
is the news of the day.

Earbob is satisfied easily and always.
The carnivores are wasted.
(Supply-Demand leaves schoolboys
hungry. There's just so much
to go around.)

Old Grunt n Groan died rushing,
massive arms locked around
his latest personal nightmare,
his skin the blue of faded jeans.

Check-out Girl draws a forty-hour
giggle every Friday.
She has earned her slice of the corpse;
so no one has to hate for her.

Bagboy?
He prospered, too,
in his own way,

injecting his own strings
until he became his own corporation
and, finally, the dividend
on his own investment.

BILLY COLLINS

Library

Here
books open themselves
words hop off their pages
forming gangs. The Verbs
slip into tiny black jackets
and stomp the helpless
                    legless Nouns.

Bad Dreams

some twitch of the pajamas
a hot fingernail

rakes the intelligence,
the lively sponge.

an arm hangs over the bedside
grounding itself like a wire.

the eyelids convulse
the mouth stares and drools.

I ride the red mare
to dawn   & all

I remember
is machine guns.

Shock

He grew up in a bathrobe
the size of Ohio

watching stringbeans
play basketball on
the ceiling of his room

staging wrestling matches
between his paunchy hands

kissing gray women
who appeared on the tv screen

loafing in furry slippers
imitating sirens

gluing and stapling
the wrong things together

getting whipped
by a tall, sane father.

Sentence

its syntax is an arrow
whizzing in the woods

splitting the apple
on your head

the two halves drop
the arrow trembles in the tree

the reverberation
greens the entire forest

it was a clean shot, perfectly
worded

you didnt flinch

TERRANCE KEENAN

Phillips Mill

Even on hills by here,
without moving a moment of water,
into grasses slip leaves like air
by rain of three days since.
In memory rain is everywhere after
men speak in whispers
that there is no release from visions.

When red berries forget names of birds
the future slips away.
Morning come behind us and mourning too,
between mint, garden, and teahouse
at the famous sea bound river.
Houses on the towpath
have been homes of men larger than rain,
on the toe path of sweet summer.
Laugh me back or cry me
to locusts and cowshit baking in the fields,
to buttercups dancing faster than the sun
and dying faster.

Home and bound
by this knowingly chosen evening
birds and berries slip like leaves.
Million whispers of rain
more wondrous than soft summer lightning.
Murmurs run over the grass
though no wind blows.
The deep and unraveled wood
is full of voices.
This much in as many different thoughts
as dusks wash away over the immense
whispers of men in the twilight,
even on the plains by the sea.

EMERY E. GEORGE

Grief

He cackled aloud at his mother's funeral
—I saw it—then went home and entertained lone grief
for a month. A drama critic, he plies his chief
trade at night; pity and fear in general
he leaves in the school books. The audience can howl,
shed tears, or laugh: he'll sit through that Shaw performance
pokerfaced and angry. What he finds enormous
are the cold, blank stares you meet in the windswept hall

afterwards. The flask of sympathy everyone bottles
until just curtain. That no one identifies
with Joan (not really); that our howls and *Ohs* are lies.
Catharsis had best be measured in aristotles,
he once wrote, as is tension in volts. That it's not life,
any more than someone's funeral is your death
(it's boredom); than tears are properly shed to Brecht.
That faces long only in public flaunt belief.

I say he is right. Today I had to attend
a funeral, prior to which there had been a mixup
of corpses. A thoroughly embarrassing event.
Of heads piously bowed in grief there was no need.
But they had to have the correct body brought in
before the burial service itself could proceed,
before the poor rabbi could even pronounce
the sacred syllables that the solemn occasion
under normally aggrieved circumstances demands.
At last there emerged reasonable mimicry
of sorrow. I dared hardly cast up a secret glance
for fear I'd face a roomful of death mask and irony.

Projects

One peers over test tubes, samples soils;
one sits with a stock of vouchers and signs.
A third stares at just-delivered designs
for a city. A fourth sees huge brass coils
emit sparks each the size of a man—
the engineers, the giant project monies, loom
menacing as cyclotrons in a room
no man will enter: neither dare nor can.

Another secret: how noted the place is
for projects the students themselves mastermind.
The giant yo-yo the seniors have designed,
built and installed as their honors thesis.
See it mounted on their one-hundred-meter
science tower there? You'll never get bored
watching it go up-down on its nylon cord.
They operate it by a small electric motor.

Yes. Those are bicycle wheels, not car tires.
Up and down it goes. Should outsiders compare
what professors do in their marble towers
with yo-yos, I'll point out: the institution fires
the radical professor from the very classroom
and hires the bum. The true-blue drone retires,
yet comes in and keeps his office door ajar,
just enough to slip out the bicycle wheel.
He will let not a one administrator bar
the kids who run the shops. And I say one admires
skill and nerve. Already you hear
that seven-foot frisbee whirring through the foyers.

Weatherman of Sorrows

The *New York Times* I buy from him each day
I leave unread. Before you think, What a fool,
visit the man. His stand is a time capsule
(a rare news-tent): its walls and air a fray
of photographs of all that's fit to print
(uneasy peace ten thousand miles away);
his knowledge of the facts his sorrow, joy;
his face scarred deep. We go on more than hint.
A cold air front is moving up through Kansas,
the prairie states (here it's about to rain),
but don't you read about it. Touch.the green
tent walls. He piles more bricks around. The canvas
pulls forty-five degrees taut, and hollow then,
his magazine-chalet camps up a storm
to shallow minds out for a thrill. A form
of newsreel! Far off you see fellow men,
Angkor ruins, mountain trails dust-pounded
on secret bombing raids. The rice turns flood
in fields the communists have long since fled —
the man's leg stump just bled. There's no compounded
mystery here: just a life we do not know.
(Don't search the sky for hints. The sky is paper;
the moon is war; his ancient face a crater
I came upon a full decade ago.)

I come this morning; his lips and nose look bashed.
A glance at headlines: six hoodlums are held
for muggings. Two old women were felled,
four hurt (a newsman near Times Square is bushed).
News breaks; he cracks. Don't let his business fold;
fold your paper instead and keep the cold
out. His face is half sunlit, half in shadow.
(The East German Foreign Ministry, madder
than Kafka, has told the secret of the Wall.
All of Berlin, Berlin is heard to say,
be viewed henceforth as split the other way:

both sides shall sample both, or none at all.)
So it goes, day by day. I can't keep up
with news and faces both, yet fill his cup.
Are we leaving the sun? The launching schedule
costs a dime. Never mind. His moonstruck eyes
study Venus; his left arm prophesies.
He counts down change, pulls back into his module.

JONATHAN SISSON

Poem

The horse in the grass.
The horse by the fence.

The lichen on the rock.
The lichen on the rock.

Nudity is no big thing with her.
She took two years to cash my check.

Wife and Mother

His habit was to counter all her questions
with 'I don't know whether to laugh or cry,'
and your divorce court or therapy session,

insisting she had most remote designs,
would put a finger on it, and would laugh,
and truth to tell she didn't much mind

as long as the car started, shape was loved,
the next year's Christmas tree was not forgot,
the law delayed and venison enough.

Her husband's child will love her, as for that.
My father told me that was his expression
and once he heard his father using it,

so if you need a lesson, there's a lesson.

LARRY ZIRLIN

When Greenberg Speaks, Can a Poem Be Far Behind?

when mother keeled over into the meatloaf
we all had a grand time trying to remove
the hardboiled egg from her nose
all of us but father
who was too busy chewing on her dress
for the last time

the family next door got angry & called the
fire department, but that didn't work so they called
an ambulance but gave the wrong address so
the-hospital-that-swoops-down-the-highway-
in-the-guise-of-a-wetdream-cadillac
crashed thru the living room wall of the folks
down the block, the ones who used to have
the three great danes but now only have one
with a gimpy leg.

listening to all the noise made me remember
the first song Mrs. Glucose, the church organist
taught me to play:
I Turn To You For Help When There's Only Hope
or something like that

the doctor gave daddy something
for Dacron poisoning
he was amazed at what an early age
i had invented pantyhose

sometimes
when the color tv won't work
we visit mommy's dress
& pour salt into all the little holes
that daddy made.

151

i waited for you all day in front of the station, 23 degrees,
snowing, waited until the newspaper vendor began making
book on how long i would stay. spent the night
waiting for your call, i thought your explanation
would be so convincing that i would forgive you
my frozen feet & runny nose, but when i fell
asleep that morning i still hadn't had the chance
to whisper "it's all right, i love you." two
days more have gone by, the mailman has
just been here, no letter from you. if
it was coming by regular post it would be here
by now, tho i have to admit i expected
a special delivery letter & stayed home
from work to receive it. ("to hell with BFW
Tool & Die" i said to my secretary, "i've got
more urgent matters") but i've got to go to work
now, you understand, i have to live my life, i'm
leaving this note on the door just in case you
arrive while i'm at work. ask my neighbor for
the key. maybe i'm fooling myself. i'll be back
around seven, i have a dentist appointment after
work. make yourself at home, there's food in
the fridge & the brand of beer you like.
i can't understand, you're not here. it's
just not like you. maybe you got hit by a
bus, or brutally murdered, or died of some
rare disease that left your beauty intact right to the end.
the last time i saw you, you *were* affecting the Ali
McGraw look, the pout, the nose, the eyebrows, but i let it
go. i'd have my secretary check it out with all the hospitals
& funeral homes if i could only remember where you
come from. meanwhile, what am i supposed to do
with the 20 piece silver setting my parents gave
us, the savings bonds from Uncle Al, the
house & car my grandfather bought? the
whole family is dying to meet you. i'm going to
have a hell of a time explaining all this, especially

to mom. it's not everyday she gets to buy a new dress. i've left my number on my pillow. call me as soon as you get in.

DAVID McKAIN

Fireflies

for Megan

At a suburban yard-sale,
I found a book called *Bird Beast & Flower:*

gold-leafed in cow-hide, colored.
I gave it to my daughter.

Drawing with magic-markers,
she makes owls from it,

deer & rabbit, the common turtle:
what stumps her is *pyralis*—

how to catch that blink at night,
its nerved-up magic timing.

After supper on the porch to watch,
I finally tell her—that wink

of light, every six seconds,
it's a sign between the sexes.

It can't be drawn to please,
it can't be done through art.

The Tremor

So diligent the work of my parents
to erase the illusions of this world,
to prepare me for a life of spiritual joy
without fay-collars, suffering, jewelry,

154

even now, twenty years later,
I still scowl at mere physical beauty:
the full, sensuous mouth, the radiant eyes—
even while feeling stirred and shaken,
pulled forward, repulsed, alive...

The Late Show

Play, let the cards and light fall
on the green and sickly table.
Twenty years have passed and I'm still
the little man grown up into the small
man with the big hat and black shirt,
my tie the color of mother-of-pearl.
I'm still the heel with the harsh tongue
who sends the pitiful imbecile out
for beer and pastrami and a gun
in a shoe-box: I'm the one who loses
and shoots out the light that makes
white-flashes on the silver-screen
go flat, go grainy like a dead Italian.

Moral Artistry

In a future dynasty of wealth and injustice,
when the Chinese again become poets,
they will read of our lives in time-capsules
and speak of the rich professionals of America
with Oriental inscrutability and awe:
how, they will wonder, did so many men
of uncommon circumstance slide so easily
into the ancient trap of spiritual depravity.
They will wonder that a land of such surfeit
had no curiosity, knew nothing of history,
of the rich merchants of Nineveh and Babylon.

When snow-caps burn through the clouds,
there will be poets like Li Po and Po Chü-I.
They will write inside the walls of lean-tos.

MARTIN STEINGESSER

Shoplifting Poetry

We're in the bookstore stealing poems,
lifting the best lines—
You cop one from Williams,
I stick my hand into Pound.
No one's looking. . .
I throw you a line from *The Cantos*—
It disappears in your ear like spaghetti.
We stuff ourselves with Crane,
cummings, Lowell, Voznesensky—
Neruda, Rilke, Yeats!
The goods dissolve in our brain.
Now we move from the shelves with caution.
The cashier's watching. Can she tell?
Fat! We've overeaten.
You giggle. End-rhymes leak at your lips like bubbles.
I clap a hand on your mouth.
You are holding my ears
as we fall out the door.

Machismo

You go to the barber.
His sign says, EXPERT TRIM.
Carefully you tell him
how you want your hair.
He says he understands,
turning your chair
away from the wall
and starting to scissor.
Curls fall
in your lap like years.
Behind, a copy of you

waits in the mirror.
The signal is given: "Through!"
Together you rise
and turn like gunfighters,
facing each other—
Into his glass eyes
you glare. . .
He is weaker than you.

ED OCHESTER

after advertising ended

small children starved to death,
mothers did not know how to lactate
and wore brassieres over their eyes,
telephone wire was cut into belts and ties,
airplanes were worshipped
and cars lathered with acne lotion;
thousands of women migrated into the Atlantic singing
and bewildered young lovers
tentatively put their thumbs in their ears.

For You

How sad to be a casual girl,
how sad to be bounced
in the rear of station wagons
along the shores of shrunken lakes.
How sad to listen to the men play
blackjack in the cabin and believe
Kafka's Castle is a hamburger joint
and Truffaut a kind of mushroom.
How sad never to understand anything at all.
How sad to walk along the lake at night
and not understand why the stars have all
been eaten by the god whose name you
forget at the moment but whom
Tibetans try to frighten with bells, cymbals,
and hideous dances on the edges of knives.
How sad to return to the cabin
and find the dead goose hung to bleed,
clamps in its nostrils, spinning
clockwise, counterclockwise;
that beautiful body hung like meat,

dribbling blood truly toward
the center of gravity.

STEVEN ORLEN

The Drunken Man

There's nothing you can say to a man who drinks.
He rises in the gray mist of morning and lights
His cigarette, knowing that soon he'll be elsewhere.
Out in the world the old men sweep their shops
And one barber nods. The full-breasted woman
Airing her pillows, she smiles and squints
And seeing it is only him, she closes the window.
But it doesn't matter. There's no way of hurting
A man who drinks. His wife floats in his pockets.
His father twists open the cap. His mother whispers
Drink, drink. He moves on down the street.

There are times when you feel obligated to speak.
You take your hands from your pockets.
You slide your glass away from him. In earnest
You'll say something—anything, the weather. . . your son—
And he'll argue at you from some place
You can't know because you're not a drunk.
Perhaps when you stagger home your wife screams
To shut up, come to bed like a man. Your face
Reddens, your shoes drop, you burrow into her flesh.

But a drunk is like a cloud, is like a ship
That sinks but never drowns, is like a feather bed.
Already it is noon. His mother and his father
Are half gone. He's weightless now.
Don't waste your pity on a drunken man.
There are too many of him, and your breasts are too few.
At night in the bar you are his weakness,
His hope and his family. If you argue back,
If you arm-wrestle him, if the bartender
Is embarrassed by your antics, it's time to go home.
Go home. Go home to your noisy wife.

161

The Jewish Family

Mother's on her bed playing solitaire,
Refusing to sleep. Why is she suddenly old
And bitter, and without sex to save her
Or pills to put her under like a little girl?

There's Father striding the huge cracks
Because nothing is wrong,
Dignified in his long coat like a paint brush
Spreading sickness, smiles and fix-it.

When we can't sleep, we roll over and over.
We make up stories to fit the bad things
And by turns we are heroes or victims.
When we can't remember, what's to become of us?

One night we decided to be heroes,
To kiss our enemies until they were Jewish.
Then the grocer refused us credit,
Then it took forever just to make mistakes.

Whose story is this? Whose lifetime?
No one's to blame. We dawdle around the table
Like wisely unattempted lives,
Totaling up our accounts: this pain

Is for Father for looking away, for frowning;
This pain is for Mother
Who keeps it inside and sickens
Into gall stones, into one lonely breast.

Remember the house, Daddy,
Bristling with sores that wouldn't scar,
And the cop who kept finding me under pillows
And porches, sooty and weeping, confessing?

Every friend I have is a hoodlum.
Every girl I take is a bad girl

With toothless parents and dirty hair
And I fall forever for our sins.

If you love me, Daddy, do it good,
Beat me up laughing, not crying
Like a sorry old man. Why is love
Like dying? Why don't we ever leave home?

First Story

Thick snow, the path, an evergreen
Hung above an ice-locked stream,
And home through the woods he found
A hand upthrusting from the snow.
His dog growled. The hand was frozen blue.
He was afraid to tell his father
Whom he told all his eager secrets,
Afraid to touch the stiff, curled
Fingers or enter the cave of palm,
But numb with winter he came back
To sit in the widening circle of story:
A man lay by a northern stream,
Lost in trout-depths, feverish.
His gashed leg refused to heal.
That night the wolf returned to snarl.

Sunday, when the others knelt in church,
He pressed the blue fire of palm
To his, and bound their hands in prayer.
He passed out in the pitiless snow.
The tree let down its branches
Over a boy who could not stay away
From the dead, or the soon to be dead,
And an owl from a story book sang
Of another world, the underground:
It snowed, and the stream froze up,
And dark clouds hid the stars.

In his dream, they were friends,
Wolf and man, under a shell of dark.

Far off in the upper world
The miraculous living moved,
And nothing ended but the day.
A father storied his son to sleep;
Children woke, and went to school.
The boy moved through them, a ghost,
Counting the unborn nails of his hand.
He heard the cold voices urging
Him back to the woods, alone.
Under the tree, a story was ending:
And when he died, steam rose
From his flesh, the wolf moaned
And ran, the body slipped under snow.

Then spring, and the snow loosed
Over rock to unveil a man's body.
He watched them wrap it in a sack
And saw that the eyes were blind,
The mouth too dumb for grief or story.
But their hands had locked, friends
One whole winter, until the stream broke
And blessed him with its cold skill.
He heard icy veins roaring underground
And didn't know the dead could live
So long, nor pain, nor numbness end.

My Father's House

Seen from a great distance
Through the morning mist, under a fathering elm,
Returning home for no good reason,
The house invites
Like those mansions framed in photographs.
Raw edges disguised by trees

And a dog activating the yard almost to drama.

It is an old home, built and built over
By my father's father in late-Victorian.
It is porched and screened-in and solid black.
In 1950 we were safe, and overslept
On Sundays behind venetian blinds.

Without a past, this house would invent us.
Each room is a small town
Settled on and favored. These are the walls
That knew their place,
This the bureau with the decal lamb
And the mirror with nothing but eyes.
This is the house that kept on growing.

I am grateful for my father's past: mine,
As a dream belongs to me, 1909.
On our walks, he points out odd memorials.
Here a horse passed everyday,
Smell the droppings! Here he broke
His leg at soccer and rode his bike home
And the darn bone
Poked through his pants. My pain!

Some people stray far from their childhoods
Into a future they never planned.
Even by continual walking
They will not return. They forget by sleeping
And love without last names.
Often I want to walk out of doors
Like a stranger, holding my own hand. . .
To be mistrusted, as when a guest
In a lapse of conversation
Turns over a globe of snow
And dreams a pleasant country scene.

Here in my father's house
The world pulls in around me like a sheet,

And I am memorizing hats in closets,
Rings in secret places, windows
Mapped with an inner shine.
Outside, gas lamps light the street,
And in the front room, gazing at a passing horse
And a man yelling *Rags! Rags!*
Building the first radio in town,
Son of a son of a son,
Waiting to hear the first crackling
Of a distant man's real voice over wire.

The Perfect One

My friend tells me I don't understand women,
A good question to ask myself in private.
Consider my suicides, my wives, who gave birth
To me daily. Under their wings I was slick
And charming. They were the coddlers who kept me.
To the shadows of their breasts I brought my grief.
But the man, the elusive one, hid his eyes and slept.

Consider the advice my mother gave me
Wheezing on her knee: "Never marry a girl
Who can't sing in your sleep." I never did.
I couldn't find her. I lay awake.
"A boy takes wives by being forcefully inept,
A man steps into a woman's life by being blunt."
But mother's gone the way of most perfection
And father turned out to be right after all.

When I was crazy I touched a tree
And asked it what it was, beyond itself.
I think I suffered a long time without knowing.

In the mornings a lady comes to rouse me.
She is not my lover, she is not my mother.
She is the future and she is desperate to please me.

When she hands me my toothbrush, I tell her:
"Wait, you are the Perfect One, I can see
Right through you." In the next bed my father writes:
"Everything will happen in its time..."

I had a dream last night in which
She came for me. "I'm not ready," I said,
But she was all smiles like the bark of a tree.

As I grew smaller, she grew more perfectly large.
Then she found it, my birthmark, and entered
My body through that one remaining hole without teeth.
"Get out," I told her, "you're just like me!"

She smelled like death as I breathed her out.
All of this is written in the book my father wrote.

No Quarter

Limping among the hookers and drunks
He tells me he's done it all,
He's done it everywhere as hunter
And hunted, his wide mouth open. Tonight
He seems boyish, his head is strangely
Large for his body: he's brooding
Because his father left the sea
For a woman and that's bad luck for a Portuguese.
Now one brother's in jail and the other
Sits banging his head against walls.

The bars along the side streets
Are slowly closing. After hours
The silences between the squares of the city
Keep us at arm's length, a kind of grace,
And the passing girls refuse his glance.

Here is his motto, he says, here is
What he means beyond the details of a life:
"No love, no loss."
                    He pauses
At the alley's mouth. He leans into
My listening face and says he's meaner
Than any man, and points
To his face for proof: the chipped
Teeth and caved-in portions
Of brow are the bad debts of a thief
Who preys on thieves. In the black alley
He searches among the tangled veins
In the scarred crook of his arm
For the path from heart to brain,
The softest sac, where there is no
Love and no loss, no temptation
To exist beyond this resting place.
He fixes me with his small, blurred
Eyes to say he's never killed
Except by accident, scared that he will,
Then whispers, "beauty rules anarchy,"
Squeezing me to show how gentle he is, my pal,
My shadow more loving than any man.

SHARON LEITER

Roadrunner and Coyote

Like the vicious cartoon innocent
I have slammed you into
every shape of nonexistence.
Obedient boulders have flattened you.
Lightning from your own hand
smashed you to a negligible ash.
As soon as the weapon fell to me,
I struck your head, your toe,
your breast, hammering some one
part of you to laughable proportions.

Like the durable pursuer,
you return, and several livingrooms away
you sit tonight,
humming your foreign harmonies
and nothing out of place.

RONALD KOERTGE

Folding The Panties

The washwater blond said that no self-respecting
man would do his own laundry much less
a woman's.

I rehearsed some face saving lines:
My wife is ill.
My old lady's sick.
My tramp is on the skids.

She interrupted, my excuses hung there
edgewise:

Your woman's not home, neither, she said.
Out with a real man, that's where she is
and you with every panty she owns right
there in your basket.

I smiled politely, strolled outside, sprinted
for a phone.

She was there all right, the crafty bitch. But
I smelled the whiskey on her breath, heard
the bed slosh and then more pairs of boots
hit the floor than I cared to count.

Getting The License

I am causing a sensation here in the County Clerk's
        crummy
office, but it is only because I am not wearing Hush
        Puppies
like my colleagues in near-groomdom. Yes, that must

be it,

there is nothing else it could be: the prancing
    Arabian stands
docile at the curb, the ocelot lies quietly at my booted
    feet,
the canaries and kingfishers are active but not noisy.
    I wonder

if it can be the salamander? I do not think so, that
    man
over there has one also, or is that his tie? No time for
conjecture now, they require our signatures. My
    child-bride

looks up at me as we swear the information given
    above is the
truth and the whole truth. I give my love a ruby for
    her smile,
hand the unmarried clerk a check for a zillion dollars
    and

shake hands all around. In each eager palm I leave a
    coin, a
gold doubloon still cold and wet from the sea. Outside
    the crowd
Ahhhhhhs as I throw her across the saddle. The
    steed whirls once,
twice and suddenly rises into the air. As we float into
    the
evening sky a million children light their matches
    and her name
appears in flame across a hundred square miles of
    wilderness. She

looks down at the speeding earth. "Yes," she says.
    "Of course,
but do you love me? Do you really, *really* love me?"
    What a

girl! I lean forward, spurring the horse to incredible
      heights.

As the galaxies spin themselves out behind us, I call
      to her,
"Look," I shout. "Look at this." I rise in my stirrups
      and—
because she wisely prefers gesture to emotion—I
      eat the moon.

YVONNE

She-Who-Opens

Suppose it is true.
Suppose the illness
knocks on your door.
Suppose you let it in.
He will probably ask you
"How much do you love me?"
You will feel a warning between your legs.
You will hear a faint buzz
or tide
somewhere in the kitchen.

But today you are less than hungry
and none of the deep sacred places
none of the secret things
you have told him
comes back to you in gossip.
He will open his wallet. A flat brown thing
you never touch. He will show you
a snapshot: A girl about four years old
blowing out candles. Two pom pom braids,
a flat moon face, the color of honey.

"My daughter."

Something inside you.
Something huge breaks and crawls into the corner.
Just who, just who is the cause of it?
Just who is wrong? Where is the tooth,
claw, the hardest lesson
a woman must track? How have you become
this small dry fire?
Somewhat less than loyalty.
More than a bed and children.

But suppose it is true.
He tells his side of it and you don't like it
But suppose it is true.
Grass, trees, water—but more voracious.
That is what you really want to be.
Unlocked. Unhooded. Hunters who know
their own smell,
who know their own killing needs.
And never blink.
And never blink.

1946

Puckering in the speckled porcelain
pot, Corinna's starch could have been
whipped white potatoes for her best
lady's prime-cut steak.
She was no less careful and determined.
Martha, the younger, came visiting
borrowing praise and her curling iron.
"Your Mary's an all right girl.
Never give me no back talk."
"Never give Spivey none before, but
good hustlin' needs good feedin' on time."

Behind schedule, a fine Christian woman,
Corinna lifted her strength
from Martha's whining, more daily than
rheumatism and more like sin.
"You suppose that's all she done wrong?"
Martha stiffened and brayed.
"All them Spiveys is crazy!
Mae Reen's an epileptic!
And my Mary don't go nowhere!
(she spoke straight as a knife)
Don't have to work nobody's kitchen but her own!"

Lifting the wide-mouthed pot,
thick-lipped cornerstone
where the base of life (until last year)
was a pot-bellied coal stove
where the flesh of life
is still hog maws, the blood
strong with sassafras tea;
lifting, setting the starch down
on the chipped drainboard to cool,
Corinna broke her peace
"My best lady died on me this Friday."

"Ain't none of 'em *that* good.
What'd she die of?"
Corinna's mind centered. Seven
white shirts piled dry as wrinkled
money. Soon they would hang
in that pale winter bathroom, in
that tumultuous bungalow, as
starched and stiff as plaster
wings for the dead.
"Old age took her.
Her eyes was flat and kind to the end."

Now Corinna wet each shirt
with a thick solid hand.
She bathed each shirt in cooked-down starch
with a grease-burnt hand.
She wrung each shirt
with a thorough hand.
She hung them on black wire hangers
wrapped with old waxed paper.
"Did she leave you what you said
she said she was gonna leave you?"
"She never said what."

Martha was quiet and looked around.
The linoleum flecked black and white
turned gray

with Corinna's faithful scouring.
Wallpaper thick with chicken fat, lard
turned blank
with Corinna's righteous scouring.
Woodwork rough with gritty
cleanser, coal stove rough
with tough white cleanser.
The ceiling was out of reach.

"Ain't none of 'em that good.
What you doin' this Saturday evenin'?"
"Ironin'."
"Ironin'?
High price for your high yallah man."
"No, he's more than a redcap, now.
And I'm his wife.
And I'm no common-law arrangement."

LORING JOHNSON

Untitled

In the mornings
smells of mint and wild onions
on the wind;

Whatever direction
the gaze is turned
you can see

discarded grooves
made by birds flying
south for another spring,

following the path
love follows;

The folds of waves in the shallows
are the faint ribs
of weight the earth knows—

tracing intricate
and idolatrous patterns
on her skin:

Unpenetrating
to beginnings or ends

I know only
the instant
between earth and sky;

and consent
to that loss
the rivers flow out to

THOM SWISS

The Pouch

When you stand it in the dark,
It slouches with the full weight
Of the vanished—this cowskin slick
With shine; this satchel of old weathers:
Stomach sagging, ruined with grief.

Last survivor of the Indian Wars:
Bag-of-Breath; its true, maiden name.
There is fringe stitched to the collar;
Around its throat, a string of beads.
The mouth is a trough
Thieves come to empty in the moonlight.

What remains when they have gone,
Is what has always been there—the wrinkled
Spirit; the pouch of all lost things:
Needle, rope, fire-flecked sheet, the spoon
With our dead brothers' medicine still in it.

CLEOPATRA MATHIS

Two Memories

Did you exist, ever?
Did I ride on your shoulders,
did you rock me as I slept?
I know you were tall and carried the weight
of three wives. And though you left us
for the fourth, your blood is mine.
It shouldn't matter, we all go on.

I have been given a memory.
The cabin where your father lived, leaning wood
on the high bank of the Mississippi.
The slope rotting into water.
Inside, two rooms divided by fireplace
for heat, mantel burdened with Bibles
and faded pictures of thirteen children.
He was a godly man, my mother says,
who took a Cherokee wife.

I can remember the smell of darkness.
I remember my sleep
with animals under the handmade floor,
the stone foundation grunting and the wind
finding the spaces between the boards.
You were there,
but I see my grandfather.
And though I open the memory wider
your face and body merge gently into his.
He is pouring molasses
the color of the winter river on a plate
of biscuits and the cold
stands stiff inside me.

Learning to Live with Friends

Like you, your house had a beauty
that rules its surroundings,
modifies itself. The ownership was clear;
you had no use for curtains, the shutters
never closed. At night, wood floors
gleamed after you. Wherever I walked
I was not alone. By day, all that white:
light gave the walls everything you wanted.
Plants breathed like children.

Up by six in the haze, we drank coffee
for hours, watered porch baskets of fuschia.
Around us the country loaned a solitude.
Endlessly our bodies darkened.
I thought how warm you looked, sulking in a blue shirt.
Later you brought out anger
and I knew its heat was old in you.

Caroline, I have seen some of your skins,
the layered dark and light that contain you
like a cloud. In a rage, you wore yourself.
Those storms left us nowhere to hide;
you claimed the rooms you screamed in,
husband following. I don't know what he offered,
perhaps some care that marriage lends.
I'm writing this because I had nothing to give
except the fear friends have.
I saw some madness in you like my own,
the one we speak of but rarely show.
That boundary is its own pain. I watched you
as I would watch myself.
Seeing us both, I turned away.

The Man on the Bed

For the woman, a braid of hair lying on the quilt
is enough. I cared for the man
and if I made him like myself, you'll understand.
When he watches her hot closed sleep
he knows their gentle house of the bed
is temporary as the ice breathing
on the glass. He pardons the future,
discarding the small lies.
See how he opens and closes his cold hand.

What matters is the way he maps the room
as it will lie years later,
just as he maps the lines in his hand.
I think he secretly cries
and wants to touch the long wall of her back.
Shall I say he's afraid
of this warning, that he cares too much
for the borders of his life?
Something else: he knows
another man will lie there, knows
and tears himself from that regret
until I whisper with him finally,
love me, love me.

Rearranging My Body

I have a woman's feel for time,
hands that know when to be innocent.
When you watch me, I am graceful
like any southern girl
who learned to yield, easily
borrowed the rhythms of walking.
Black women washed my skin
and showed me when to leave well enough alone.

Now this changes; my mouth widens.
I am wild with hair. I strip
off this cotton dress, tear apart
my legs that will learn their own time.
I open my crotch and reach inside.
My stomach becomes a new fist;
I rearrange the obedient fingers of my ribs.

You'll see my body,
the new hard curves
of a woman bent over in a soybean field.
You'll smell the overcooked greens,
the brown sweat. Even now, see my wrist,
the underside thin and pale
as a fish's belly, the veins
strong as catgut.
I am no longer familiar. It is all right
if you never want me again.

DOUG FLAHERTY

For a Girl Whose Slow-Dying
Called for My Blood

Days full of sunspots the girl
surveys the seeds of her garden

joyfully fingers the pumpkins
initialed with neighbor men

growing beneath her touch
She opened into bloom

like Rappaccini's daughter
flowering on poison

Rose thorns bled the sun white
while she pricked her finger

touched the tip of a clematis
posing like God Father and Eve

in holy paintings of creation
Her eyes know god is blood

why everyone's horned crazy
frighted by visions of werewolf

And when no one visits the sea
the girl with no color

sketches faces of men
on smooth oval stones

Behind her for miles
hundreds of cast-off faces

drown in the incoming tide
A man in white carts her away

drains off her blood
and injects the hope of strangers

R.T. SMITH

Solo Late Show Over Easter Break

(for Lorn)

You smoke pot alone in your room.
Stoned, you roll down to the movies
for the late show, where a ticket allows you
the same rights a ticket allows anyone, by God.
You swallow popcorn nearly whole through shorts
and wait for the great porn show
with the dozen or so other denizens of the mezzanine
scattered like buckshot in their overcoats.
BARBARELLA bounces bosomy across the screen
in outer space copulation, and out of the corner
of your eye you spy your nearest neighbor in the
anonymous dark: his hand flies to his crotch and
buttered fingers scrub his pecker like
an anatomical mushroom he's cleaning for the soup.
(With such dairy product lubrication,
he needs not fear he'll rub it raw.)
You squint your ears and hear
such stroking all around, its almost like the crew race:
the sound of one hand clapping, outlaws' muffled applause.
Well, the psychedelic lights flash in kaleidoscopic
carnival of carnal delights and Jane Fonda climaxes
in colors and sighs float up from the watchers
like souls from bodies of the newly dead.
(Remember the sci-fi orgasm of Jon Voight in MIDNIGHT
COWBOY when Bob Balaban (you heard me!) went down on
him on Forty-Second Street? Of course you do.)
When the house lights come on and all the phoenix heroes
with their juice-sweet boxers stalk, hands in pockets,
out onto the snow-shrouded streets to auto away,
you notice a dampness in your pants' lap and hurry home
to your wife. Or anybody's wife.
It's nearly two o'clock on Sunday morning.
He is risen.

185

Angels We Have Heard on High

On Christmas Eve we drove
back up the spine of the Blue Ridge
saw in the road a black dog
small as a cat—with two broken front legs
he limped across the highway
just then a train—westbound—boomed
in black iron thunder

I imagine my ex-wife and her lover
tossing late in the storm

our hands are bound with barbed-wire
nobody gets what he wants

(like thunder)

DAVID CHILDERS

Hunt

We fashion spears
from the forest
for Harrisson's pigs
gone wild. All day
we follow tracks
over creek beds
rocks and stump
jutted hills.
Farther away
from the fences and town

Our water turns
tepid. Our bodies
smell rank. We
smoke and curse and wait

Until the dogs get crazy
in the late glow
looking deeper through
the shade while
the moon comes up
white and early like
an O on our mouth

When the tracks take form
on a high mound of
stones and the spear
strikes unseen bone
as the wild roar
pierces the wood.

We rest with our
tracks behind us.
Trees bend against

the change of sky.
We rest on a poem
in the blood
on the ground.

South Carolina Baptismal Procession

                Below the hawk
           beside the hulks
                 of rotting river barges
             white forms
carry torches
    Songs
    from the sun
             and the night thick
                      soul
             wind over water
    green
    with snags
    and hand like
           leafy shadows.

                      Look down O Lord
                      Look down
from your golden Heaven
in the tall tree tops.

            Under the quarter moon
          upon the moon pale sky
      the preacher
    dances chanting
             "Rise up
             Rise up
             Rise up
        again to live
         to see

to hear!"
                    The following replies
     "Rise up!"
               Laughing
               they go
          along the longer
          river shore
                    into the deeper
                         night.
                                   Look down
          O Lord look down
                         from your silver
                         strip of cloud
                         across the dusk
                         horizon.
                                   Look down
from your hidden
wanderings
          and misty
     ways.

CHARLES O. HARTMAN

Mastodon

> To sculpt an elephant, chip from a large block
> anything that doesn't look like an elephant.

He fell and was drowned too far
from where the confrère dinosaurs
basked in their tar-pits
to decompose in peace. He froze
before he could drown, and merely slept
snug in a new block of the pole's building.

And while he slept he became extinct.
He began to wonder, in his glacial way,
being kept so long in nature's antechamber,
whether he was ignored or just forgotten,
and by whom. Who was left?
He forgot.

When the little fellows he remembered
as busybodies with stone-chip spears
attacked the ancient ice and laid him bare,
he found himself so exhausted with waiting
as to have forgotten the protocol.

He could not play the old game, stamping about
trumpeting while they pelted him with brickbats;
for who would not, having lived so long
protected from the passions of the sun,
functionless, ill at ease, wish
merely to rise and step again
into the fumbling hands of the sea?

A Prayer for Violets

On the window-sill across the alley
there are always shoes, old shoes
with tall thick heels. The old woman
rotates them like crops; every pair
is black, scuffed gray.
                              At night
her television blares across to us.
Its gray light affronts the moon.

One afternoon while the light turned gold
my wife was bringing in from the fire escape
our rose bush in its redwood tub.
The woman's face glimmered above the shoes
and called out, "Where are you taking
my garden?"
                   Tonight
she is a shape like a heap of stone fruit
in that flickering light, waiting
for God to come on and tell her
the sacrifice is approved, the shoes
will ascend tomorrow in a golden shaft.

But this evening, when the foxfire
ages the shoes and freezes the old woman,
I put my book down and lean toward the window
and pray that God will leave the shoes,
unpolished, filled heel to toe with good loam
and thick with violets drinking the moonlight.

To Shadow

Noon sets the tips of pines on fire;
trunks' shapes are half-guessed. The goshawk's
claws glint among ragged feathers.
My feet trace out the hurried way.

191

When the field and its winding path
answer no question, pose nothing,
my stride slows; easy light casts down
the tree behind me till, a shade,
I wind through the branching shadow.
Evening's levelling everything.

When I see the hawk's smooth winging
home, it seems the world lays down arms
forever. (Hunched in the thick grass,
a blind spot swimming in this blind
repose, a mole thrusts through its long
labor, through this short peace of night.)

Light wears thin. I hear doves whistling
in the dark. On the wide field, day
lies down to sleep, a man worn dark,
his own shadow's weary hunter.

Before My Father Before Me

My mother's mother painted her
Perhaps in 1936
At perhaps thirteen
In the tentative light of a White Mountain dream.
The house not shown
Is sold to strangers now.
It might be raked leaves the color of her hair
She watches, flushed.

Her high and silken blouse is the same
Blue-green as the mountains,
A color almost of sea.
In 1936 her eyes,
Half as old as when I met them, half

As old as I am now,
Were dry as leaves,
Bright as the scattered leaves.

My grandmother nearly always painted trees.
In this there are only mountains, things
Keeping their blue distance.

The old lady is dead. Her brush
Made these mountains of a half-known mother's wish
Or set them down as they were by her daughter's eyes
Composed of vague desire and the sea.

She dreams of distance
Hazy and wide as the North Atlantic,
Peopled with strangers;
Holds it still as she holds her blazing
Head for her mother's brush.
Between pale lips she
Breathes the world that invests her
Into being,
Formless,
Perfect:
A woman with my own face,
Thinking of other things.

Milkweed
for Howard Nemerov

Milkweed is pertinent now; so in the air
That everyone is thinking in its terms.
The housewife doesn't dare hang out the wash
Without considering milkweed; engineers
Decide today to redesign the air
Filters they thought perfected. It's a fact:
Milkweed has come to live and be lived with.

Reprieved, the birds have ceased to pluck their breasts
To line their nests—though few enough are still
Preparing for eggs when milkweed starts to hatch,
Exploding from its brown sun-brittled pods.
Occasional nestlings get mistaken meals,
Beakfuls of milkweed someone took for bugs:
Like anything in the air, it seems all things

Eventually, a faery's shuttlecock
As soon as seeds from not the prettiest plant.
Step in a cataract of light on a day
Like this, look up and see another race
Cast from its place and looking for its place;
Riding the wind toward distant, solid ground,
They scatter golden light on their scattered way.

MARISHA CHAMBERLAIN

No Respect for Authority

While Mom and Dad
sip their evening wine
in the low, white livingroom,
the giant teenagers
return from play rehearsal
with three friends.
Politely bowing and introducing,
trying to be graceful,
they fill up half the room,
even crowded together.
"Don't get up, Mr. and Mrs.
Chamberlain, all we want
is a drink of water."
For the next three hours,
the tap is constantly running,
Dad has an ear trained to the
pump in the basement.
In another while, two of them
stoop through the doorway
and proudly present the parents
with a nice bowl of popcorn.
Each popped kernel is the size
of a grapefruit and dripping
in butter. The bowl itself is
too big to fit on the coffee table,
the parents ask for
it to be placed on the floor,
decline the gallon tumblers
of cherry limeade.
The guests go out the back
door at eleven,
ripping the porch off the
outside wall as they step
out under the stars,

never looking back and not
meaning any harm.

LYNN STRONGIN

Multiplication

How can I be wheeled down these white corridors
23 years after, without touching your hand?
brightening, diminishing:
tawny-girl in lacecap of sunlight:
Movement without memory is insanity: you are
planted in tapestry:
a cobalt flower.

Your 12-year-old-hands held the reins
of death surely, your eye aflame:
While cancer went about its multiplication
exact as lace, or honeycomb.

They cut off one leg
but it reached the hip:
indigo wore you down.
(We'd close our eyes, to picture cobalt-gardens.)

Your cheeks some days were bone-white
like the girl of Dresden holding our silk lampshade
back home:
other days, they were pink like those planted in quilts:

Rose, a North Renaissance girl.
Near the close of your life
your face was pearl: milky-grey,
it glowed in all that brightness by the window:

a nun of 12, determined, not angry,
whose sole task was to meet your king.
Cobalt-gardens multiplied, then. A sole visitor,
an aunt brought you a furtrimmed jacket for your
diminished frame.

You grew up three years overnight, & were a Vermeer
young woman: (the Dutch wear such jackets in wintertime
to keep out the damp cold of Delft Holland:)
the windowpane threw lemon light on your jacketed frame.

Hoarflowers formed in the glass—
multiplying, multiplying, until by ice-tables, they covered
you & me both with lace of a cream-white curtain
celled by snowflake bright incarceration.

RACHEL HADAS

Trial

I   The Prosecutor, a Cretan

With your permission, gentlemen,
let's reconstruct that night.

Moonless. Before her stretched the sea. To eastward
glimmered the lights of Platanos, Spatharay.

Westward the mountain blotted out the stars.
At such an hour all in Ormos were sleeping,

but she cautiously paused to listen at the door.
Only cicadas. Gasoline can in hand,

intrepid for a woman alone in the dark,
she stepped across the threshold, crossed dark space

between the house and factory (fifty yards?),
then climbed the wall. At this point I surmise

the deed was done. Small flames would have been licking
the walls as the sky blushed towards Turkey. Back in bed,

she was up in her nightgown when the alarm was given.
Convincingly upset, but not enough.

Now two years later she is in the dock.
The proof of her guilt, gentlemen, to me:

how could this woman have been happy here
among you doltish Samians?

II Sitting with Fellow Defendant

Sometimes your fellow prisoner almost becomes
                                        a confessor.
"Darling" (he takes you in his arms again)

"I'm sorry I've used up these years of your life."
"Oh love," you say, "oh yes, my love, I need you."

There was a time when you were more
to each other than fellow captives;

a time whose memory is all but gone
in this sucking slough of need.

How to remember? We scrounge and hoard our strength,
all energies scraped thin to last it out.

We last it out diminished.
The weight of this slow passage has pressed me down.

Head hanging, I'm accused by those in power
of being who I am. Of being here.

They're right, of that I'm guilty as can be.
Nor can appeals be lodged for time lost, life.

My innocence escaped them so they charged me.
My mitigating misery acquits me.

III Innocent

Pain of relief explodes, a flashbulb
only inside my head. The world dissolves

to be put together later a new way
when all this has receded far enough.

"Perástika," they say—may it pass for you—
when only now has it passed. I'll never understand.

How our burden defines us
even after its lifting off our shoulders.

Nor do I understand why next day
we are back at the scene of the crime.

But the sense of occasion takes command as usual,
the villagers gather for...yes, congratulations.

An old man, dirt in the wrinkles of his neck,
presses forward from a stable:

"The trial, my children? It's over?"
Deaf as a post, he has somehow learned the news.

That will be what they remember about us.
And of our years here, full of light and air,

at this moment I think that I will take with me
only this ending, but I will be wrong.

LEMUEL JOHNSON

from *Hand on the Navel*

Part V

and when you have after all this
been cursed and damned
and cannot shoot a white man
yourself, good lord let
the latin priest come with
his fine ululantems with
his sempiternal ululantems
and when you wrestle with
women keep the fingers close
in the quick of their
breasts rising in the
passion of a salt sweat
and let the latin priest come with
his ululantems and think you
in an ecstasy of fine crucifixions
and think you then of the slaughter
of birds and the sempiternal rot
of their hot entrails—*radex malorum*
the root of all evil is the devil's
claws but keep you your fingers
on hot breasts, remembering the fat
god who sits openthighed
by the Chindwin river and you will
dance the dance of the bent knees
standing at ease.

XXXIV

from a height of gargoyles and waterspouts
it was the bullets came skipping in high octaves
here is no last judgement, *effendi,*
only choice pieces of the heart

the quick sopranos came singing
a tart intent
     I saw them
in their long processions

may god the father damn
your arse, lieutena' of the day, but
I saw them in their long processions.

and he talked then of the meticulous craft
of pillbox hats on passionate women
in Irrawady

or perhaps much later
it was with a *madamasel* open-legged
against a strong wall

XXXV

and we came caught in the dance
of a rabble of small sorcerers
madamasel keep us in mind

and may god the father damn your arse
and may god the son damn your arse
and may god the holy ghost damn your arse
quick quick
and let the latin priest go stiff
let him go
for who born you after all?

XXXVI

ah, ah
up to now madamasel can't *pe-le-le-le*
you a man more wicked than Hitler
putting madamasel on a wall
look man how she can't *pe-le-le-le*
no more

(he came back with a cut stone
from under a cathedral
on it was a woman rode a He-Goat
to tempt the appetite
the rough forelegs of cloven hooves
erect with a stiff passion)

and look how she can't *pe-le-le-le*
no more, a deadweight against the heart.
the dry skin aches
and the pregnant mountainside does
not now open in
the invocation of this or that mere word.
one dies of stan-
ding for too long at attention;
the long years then
will not save us from barbarisms
whether or not
you lift stoppers from rich repertoires of scented flagons
what they serve here
deadens the brain, leaves the teeth naked and on edge.
the dry skin aches
for alchemic sublimations of dead stone.

XXXVII

a small finger curves outward
from fine tea in a porcelain teacup

the saucer lies, herb-scented

perhaps the bloodstained earth loves us a little
the heart beats with blood
and you put an arm around the graceless
bones of a small waist

the radio saying so
in the king, my lord's chamber.
outside the tongues of grass
stiffen in thin-sharp whispers

a great stone holds down the underthings
of a woman drowned in the river
(the radio saying so)
                     and would you
indeed have maimed yourself
not to serve—a swollen scrotum carried about
in a wheelbarrow, perhaps?
the smell of a goat about you?
or perhaps a hoarse cough of great heat
(a pink-rich throat in full song
over the white cliffs of Dover?)

and these pointless bones
were once meat cooked in an oven, did you know?
in a Rhineland forest

so you speak now in a low voice
your fingers over your lips.
too many things roam through our nights
the statue of Cecil Rhodes, for example,
standing in the middle.

XXXVIII

timmini yimre
           so the song is sung.

you wipe a hand on the navel
and talk of a relationship deeper than enmity:

a fly crossing the sky holds no meaning
nor minute skulls of foetuses
stretched across an imprecise horizon.

and what is a nugget of fact
in queen victoria days:
two englishmen shaking hands

in their presumption of
a dead continent
the bearers cropheaded and silent

in queen victoria time;
two ewes and a ram guard
the corners of paradise

in a potful of blood
the lake unnamed waits
to be named victoria.

XXXIX

the landscape is not an austere one—
for what of Circe, with illustrations?
an anxiety of hurdy gurdies
and musical boxes unseaming the aching brain
happy days are come (again)
and, man oh man, there come a tavern
in a town, you know.

in queen victoria day
good lord tell me—
she get rings on she fingers
fine bells on the toes.

look a lady ride a cock
horse and we are not ever
the owner of our days
the queen turn sunlight
to moonlight in
queen victoria time
look a lady keep she breasts
shaped like a long ewer,
full one, and I ask you,
man, when she take she leave, man,
(looking a lady)
you laugh behind your sleeve?

a fleeting ornament
on a nacreous throat.

and even that precise moment
holds no meaning, you know.

XL

and what price the statue of a victorian man
in the middle of a continent? such knowledge.
it does little good to threaten us
in high marble.
                        in nineteen twelve
you remember a ship going down
in disregard of icebergs—and
such knowledge! my mother weeping
for fine people gone to water.
legends of a childhood, I ask you!

for fete and bacchanal
nearer to god, you say?
for a people's carnival
is it rickets alone keeps a man's legs bowed?

in fifty-three they coronate a queen 'bet'
and who the devil going to stop the carnival
you bound to jump and shake the brain bone
in a hot damn carnival

in 'fifty-three they coronate a lady
in a coronation
and you in delegation
well I ask you! in a westminster chamber
how you manage, brother, to climb Jacob's ladder?

is it rickets then

XLI

how you manage till you reach
such knowledge: in his one vowel
you hear now a Qawashgar Indian sing
in a still photograph, grained with age

let them kill the Qawashgar Indian too
O that too is one way, a need perhaps.

keep to yourself and
leave the Magellan Strait to go
where it goes toward penguin and snow.

the universe is unsatisfactory
and seeks the face of a knight
toxic with armor and quick thrust.

XLII

and to what end aim a dry root
at italian carrara, thinking
of villas and fine pissoirs?
Mussolini died upside down.
and Rosa posed with a dulcimer
in Venice. for us. You remember
that picture. in Florence.
what can a dry root do among them
in Venice the stones suck a green misery sinking
so far now from Ethiopia
and to what end? to have come
this far with irregular steps, marching,
to what doxologies does one pander
now? Nijinsky danced and went mad,
did you know? at the end.

XLIII

and what shall I do back in Frankfurt?
visiting Frankfurt, a superior guest
at a prussian wedding of coyly-turned anecdotes:
do you remember the senegalese soldiers
flamboyant in cape and gas? do you?
and when they ask warum sagen sie "fromage"
they have you by the edge of the trousers!
and you are embarrassed into another age,
shaking a foreleg, embarrassed as
not even a dog can be embarrassed.
(and Spengler toxic with melancholia!)

I shall go about their cobbled walks,
let the girls ask was willst du?
in the film they will say
it was not bullets killed the beast
was willst du then? was it beauty?

a deadweight shored up against *tomorrow*
just you wait and see

XLIV

we have returned too
to France. there is a cathedral
in Marseilles flaked in gold
the dead drift of the sea below.

I remember the stone steps.
and I shall go on living, for a change,
an iron cross on my khaki.

I am not one to be like Flaubert
my every line the coffin of a dead illusion.
I go on living. the girls come.
in the cantinas I hear them eating roses

in their time or in the quicksteps of blood
they will tell me secrets of the timber
supply of ancient Rome. or Greece, perhaps.
such knowledge—the musical bones of gentle succubi
and I shall live and study the magic of the tango.

shut the blood's gate.
I have seen the sign on a fence:
this is the land of dogs and flies
shut the blood's gate
and keep out the dogs

and I shall yet revert to myself in late afternoon
tilts of the head. posed. just so.
like a cockatoo creting while
(before my time?) the river foams with small bones.

HENRY PETROSKI

From the Observation Deck, Austin

I

A picket fence of steeples to the east;
Fraternity houses off to the north;
Plate glass windows reflect us from the west;
And senators watch us from the south.

Our campus now is bounded. All around
Our universe a city grows beyond
The hills and the river and the black ground
Where cotton was and children once had gone.

Old homes beneath the trees are almost lost
In fields of oak, pecan and cottonwood;
The banks of Congress Avenue now rise
Above the Colorado and the Capitol.

Between the city and the city's soul
The highway from everywhere rises up
And hides the ghettos in the shadows that grow
Forever longer, but never long enough.

I see new houses with their open roofs
So far up north among the stunted trees
For centuries in caliche. Their roots
Are shallow, and their branches hold few leaves.

II

Here there are deeper roots, and greener trees
Have many names, many branches, many twigs
And many greens of many-sided leaves.

All roofs are red tile; walls are orange brick.

All roofs are red—Philosophy and Art
Are one with Law, Biology and Speech.
All walls are brick—Humanities and Math
Are one with Anthropology and Greek.

Concrete and dirt connect the Library
To Business, Music and the Women's Gym.
The paths are straight as a cat's cradle's string
Between ten fingers—and even more than ten.

From here the campus is a harmony of proofs
Of its existence as a universe;
Beneath the uniformly tiled roofs
There is a uniformity of shapes:

Rectangles, rectangles, rectangles, squares,
Some modified capital letters: L,
A U, a T, a stadium O,
An octagon auditorium—*Stop.*

III

I hear no lectures here, I see no halls
of open contradictions and closed doors
Of men and women in separate stalls
Considering graffiti, and a course.

I see no faculty, I hear no chalk
Scratching calculus on a palimpsest
Abandoned by a botanist whose talk
Of flowers was stopped at *Lupinus.*

I hear no bells, but now the concrete moves
Beneath a permutation of the class
of undergraduates. (Graduates move
Beneath a single roof from first to last.)

I see no mortarboards, but someone must
Be counting heads and measuring the brains
Of future contributions to the trust
That stuffs alumni in the stadium.

I hear a babble: still the blameless blame
The vertical for the confusion among
The horizontal. Yesterday I came
Up here where the wind is the only tongue.

NEIL BALDWIN

Gaining, with departure

And so it must be
in the final stillness
where not one tree
whispers denying
heated colors by
their sole vividness
marking season

My belief suffers
from interference:
every layer of
clothing approaches
a new temper
but we defend
our distance

One moment
a leaf is let go
pantomiming
the end of things

while I see it
not unheralded

Allowing that leaf
a dull departure
I would give in
to a force swaying
me the way pine
tops sway now

I will hold on and
hook imagination's

teeth to whatever
green orange yellow

or gold
offered me

D.C. BERRY

An Epistle to Celia

When I see thee, wilt thou hock,
Or arms akimbo, piss thou bolt-upright?
That, my love, that?
Or snot thy nose?
Thy pretty little nose?

O when I see thee
Wilt thou breathe a morning mouth in my face?
Hack a hag's cough, drop thy Preparation H?
That, my love, that?
Or scratch thy bum?
Scratch and scratch thy pretty little bum?

When I tell thee I love thee,
Wilt thou promise me that
A little post-pubic drip
Streaks thy briefs?
That thou dost strain at thy stool?
Tug and strain at thy pretty little stool?

Signed, thy foole.

To the Woodville Depot

> Ashes to ashes
> And dust to dust,
> If the women don't get you
> The whiskey must.

I

They let the children out of school
Every year the day
Grandpa Hays and the dogs
Drove his 500 hogs, teeth and hooves
Popping kudzu and copperheads,

216

To the Woodville Depot.

II

Davy, my flower connoisseur,
Placed a daffodil on the garbage can
Before I took him to nursery school.
That afternoon his hands
Held the shriveled daffodil.
And his lip turned up a soft,
Terrible tusk of petulance.

III

I am between the two,
Wailing and singing
To Grandpa Hays long dead in Hays Hollow
And to Davy not so much
Unborn as in another time,
But they do not hear me,
Nor does the ambulance driver
When through my whiskey lips
I tell him Lord God driver
Let that siren wail,
For we are on the way to market!
We are all that way, driver,
Let her scream.

IV

Yeah, that's it driver....You see!
You see there! The children at the curb!
The teachers behind them turning flips
And banging tambourines! Cartwheeling!
That's us they are dancing for, driver,
So let that siren sing, driver,
And that bloody light on top
Sling a bucket of blood
For every bottle of booze
Old man Hays turned butt up
Till it made the ragged flesh on his neck
Finally buck up bristle welts,

The slack meat fall off his mouth
To let his teeth crack
The heads of snakes and roots
Crawling up the dreams that held his legs in weeds
Day and night, week after week—
Music squealing from the snout.

V

So let that siren sing, driver,
Let her sing, for me, for old man Hays,
And for the child there
Holding the limp daffodil clubs,
Davy there, marble-eyed
At the sight of so much dancing and death
In the dust of Woodville Depot.

DENNIS TRUDELL

Avenue

He is walking along in his mind
and he is walking down the street. At

a right angle to his direction, ten yards away
from his library book, a thin man
is about to cross a rug. The thin man

is pale from lack of sleep; he has watched television
for nine straight hours. Behind the television

is another parlor where a blonde typist
has just stepped out of her clothes.
She turns a slow circle—but the eyes

on the poster of the black assassin stare past her
to a window whose pane shudders slightly
at a passing truck. The truck has eight

wheels and is driven by a man whose kidneys
have ached since Schenectady; the pain

makes him want to swerve toward the fat nurse
waiting at the curb with her employer's groceries.
She is thinking about her sister, who did not

send a birthday card. Between her and
the green newspaper stand on the opposite sidewalk

comes a man in denim; he is carrying a book
and needs a haircut. Then a long truck hides him,

and a small car moving the other way blocks
some letters on the truck's side. In the car
is a dentist on his way to have a tooth drilled

by a rival. His palms are moist. His car radio
announces the time and temperature, although the one who

speaks them does not think of the numbers
as his lips move. He releases them into the oblong shape
between the turntables while fighting back

the old impulse to whisper "fuck"
across the city. His mother wanted him
to stay in Indiana. His girlfriend keeps a poster

of a black man in leather. Her neighbor has been awake now

for forty-seven hours; he clicks off
the three puppets and walks into the bedroom.
He swallows fourteen capsules. In the distance

sirens begin screaming toward some pedestrian
whose large left toe has been crushed by a ton

of license plates from a penitentiary near Albany.
Two blocks away a young man turns his
back on the air and enters a library.

Epilogue

I have just joined a raggedy line
of refugees at dusk. It is raw weather;
the day was a foul wet breath. Tonight
may bring the first snow: if not, tomorrow.
The land is flat—treeless, mud.

These people are carrying things. Children, blankets.
Saucepans, poultry, books. Some are crying,
some are very old. None are fat. And one
is falling. Most are silent in several languages.
They have read no newspaper in months.

220

They are waiting to cross a bridge.
By dawn there will be fewer;
by noon there will be more.

A Locale

My brother the air in this room: I was not
like this yesterday: where were you?

My brother the football games this
week: back and forth, back and forth: and
mattering so much to my brother the wives the
men behind cigars in prisons loading bathtubs.

My brother the truth I did not tell the man I was
afraid of that spring: still here still tasting
sour: I'm sorry mister you'll have to hear it

from my brother the hard surfaces of your
city or my brother death: the way he creeps into
our shoes at night and one morning won't

retreat into the leather. My brother
the crocodile who just nosed into the brown

thickness of some river at the sound of my
brother the strange bird who now leaves there.
My brother the laws of electricity.

My brother the only stomach I'll ever carry:
I'm sorry: do you think you might try a little harder?

The molecules in the cat's tail. Causing it to
be held my brother upright tonight. My
brother the atoms of what we call "sink".

Existing in this pimple of time my brothers.

221

Along the flanks of such an immense
pale herd of it. My brother that sentence.

My brother the dreams currently at play
along this block: good luck or bad.

My brother the God I don't believe in: I love you
when you shine through the eyes of men: you bastard why

occur as a Slim Jim when I always
order Beer Nuts: heh heh: hi pop. My brother

the degree of tilt to the earth's axis: what can
I say? My brother irony, whom I cling to
while he eats me.

My brother pain: overflowing tonight my brother
the aunt the broken deer the torn tree the bruised
word the pale aunt there in the ward the
brother silence squeezing at her the brother moon

wailing at the starving piranha waiting my brother below
my brother the scent of my brother the fruit my
brother the distance my brother the
breeze has my brother bridged: Oh I

die again tonight my brother only
half-serious again brother yes and only half
here or there or any moment's unfeigned brother.

ROLLY KENT

Hanging Clothes

Whenever the president of some country speaks,
when there are riots in Boston and Tokyo
and the hunger of whole continents
stares from the empty carton,
I get out the dirty laundry
and carry big baskets of wet clothes
down to the line.

I hang a little dress, a sunsuit, my pants.
I take my time with a nightgown, a blouse, some tights.
I pat the air in panties, let the bras and hankies
fill up like spinnakers and when
the clothesline is fitted out
I sail around the dungarees to the Orient
for cinnamon and to the South for hides and coffee.
I bury my face in shirts and breathe
an ocean of chemise and scarf.
I travel through the pajamas
and trade underpants with the Islanders,
at Casablanca, contraband and smoked goat,
and in the Baltic I drink till my socks are dry.

Along the rivers and near the wharves, in alleys and backyards
through the late afternoon I think of the size
of this world, think of all its breasts
and proud crotches, its stained armpits
and strained or slender throats, think of
the muscle in sleeve and leg and the arches of feet,
I think of use, the whitegoods
shining with the shadows of trees.

The flies circle my head. Everything's
plain as sheets.

I take my time.
The towels and jeans
will be hard and sweet with sunlight.

The Old Wife

for JBB

I was the choice of many old men when I was young.
My husband was proud to give me—
whenever I lay with the old men, he said, buffalo
would come.

The first old man I lay with, I thought only of the honor.
Later on, I used to giggle, those heaving old bellies!
I went to the lodges of seven of them, seven different years,
and only once did a man not lay with me.

He wasn't like the other elders. The village
suspected him because he kept to himself.
I quaked as I walked behind him, afraid I would
not be pretty.
The bed floated in a circle of silver.
There was no place for a scared girl to hide,
so I turned my back to him and let my things fall away.
I felt him looking as I slipped beneath the robes.
Then he sat down beside me and lit a pipe.
He never took his eyes from me or spoke a word,
and I fell asleep confused with waiting.

In the morning he was still there, only
dressed now in beautiful white skins.
When I sat up I saw that I too had new clothes on,
soft skins with bead-work the colors of day.
I pulled the robes over my head, ashamed.
When I thought him gone, I popped up.
He was still there. He took my head and rubbed
fine-scented bear oil on my hair, smiled, and let me go.

Later, people thought him a wealthy man,
I a lucky girl. My husband was the envy of the village.
I lied for my looks and told my sisters
what a sweaty old bull he was.

For several days after, no one saw him.
Then some hunters found him frozen up on a hill,
watching for the herds to come, dead in the same clothes.

For a long time I made sense of that old man
by thinking I brought him what he needed before
                                                he could die.
It has cost me my body to know I was wrong,
that when he smiled, it was for an ignorant girl
who would wake up one day, a cold day like this,
feel someone's hands make her hair shine again,
and find just the sun on a dry, old head.

BRUCE BENNETT

The True Story of Snow White

Almost before the princess had grown cold
Upon the floor beside the bitten fruit,
The Queen gave orders to her men to shoot
The dwarfs, and thereby clinched her iron hold
Upon the state. Her mirror learned to lie,
And no one dared speak ill of her for fear
She might through her devices overhear.
So, in this manner, many years passed by,
And now today not even children weep
When someone whispers how, for her beauty's sake,
A child was harried once into a grove
And doomed, because her heart was full of love,
To lie forever in unlovely sleep
Which not a prince on earth has power to break.

PETER FRANK

On the Death of My Beard

In the wisdom of teeth, you are king.
Memories within memories within memories...
The lips of the palm fall off into the ocean,
and in them is poison, each one.
I forget that when vines
drape themselves over the roofs of cloisters
—legend goes—
the bears all come out to practice their largesse,
the stains run away with the flags.
In the wisdom of my teeth, you are the king.

In the wisdom of the teeth, you are my king.
Later on it begins to rain.
Why don't we take up where we left off?
Scylla and Charybdis live down the street.
I have broken through the sparrow net
and am being caught by a team of carillons.
In the kingdom of teeth,
you are caught unawares.

DAVID KIRBY

The Short Paean of Simon Forman the Astrologer:
To Tronco, His Wife

He discovered sex in 1582 at age 30, referring
to it with the code word *halek*.... Occasionally
he varies *halek* with *halekekeros harescum tauro.* I
suppose this should be translated as "Wow!"
—*The New Republic,* February 22, 197₅

For years they came to me, these hurtful wives.
The list of their infirmities was long:

Red throat, lame leg, sore back, bad tooth, tired eye,
Thin blood, loose stool, the wage of venery,

The irksome jest that nature plays each month
("It's like the tide, it can't be helped," I said).

Each was lovely in her pain and some,
If faithful in their ways, were willing:

Emilia was one, who wished to know
Of her goodman's chance at court, the while

Suggesting that I had a chance at her.
A fool, I paused. Time passed, and she turned cool.

The year of 1582 was when
I first essayed to halek with a dame

And after that it was halek halek
Until I came at last to her who is

My wife, my love that I have called Tronco,
This talismanic name I made, Tronco,

228

Incantatory name, it rhymes, Tronco!
With halekekeros harescum tauro.

I Haven't Forgotten T.S. Eliot

When you're daydreaming
and you think up these Anglo-Italian aristocrats
and give them names like Bothwell-Contini
and pose paradoxes for them,
that's the Eliot in you.

At night, when the neighbor
walks by your window and you turn, stonefaced,
to the woman who lies with you
and say "that's Sir Judas Stukeley
with his bag of traitor's gold,"
that's the Eliot in you.

And when you attitudinize,
when you turn off the t.v.
to whisper something historical,
remember: you can't forget your culture
and that, old possum buddy,
is the Eliot in us all.

JANE GARLAND KATZ

Dressing for Our Spring Party

The geese are going to live again.
Even now, while you're combing your hair
many of their dark bodies
stir beneath the mulch; I hear the enormous motion.
They turn among the roots like fists
of buried people burrowing skyward.
The trembling of the rushes is a sign from the geese
wrestling with the bulbs underground.

Come to the window. I can help you
with the cuff link. If you come
to the window you'll see them rise
there by the weed stalks; they are waking.

Forget the mirror, bring your tie out here.
These geese of the field
get wild as tornadoes, flipping
in the air with the laughter and screaming
of friends, friends who meet once again.

Some will be left behind
where the ice never completely melted
from the mud pits. The spring riot we hear
comes to them through the blanket
of milky ice. This choir
excites those who failed.
Let me lie down for a minute.
Soon, the music.

Photograph of the Hanging Pianos

The plan was to go after the city

where bells are loaded on buildings
and snow with its blue fall
brings dogs that are hungry to the street.

The stranger who takes care of you
used to sing in this city.

In the warehouse near an iced up river
pianos are hoisted on locked pulleys.
The water wind is playing them now.
The groaning of these hunchback things

goes through town like fear, above all bell ringing
and people make a promise to the good voice.

But you have not been happy here.
Even with a postcard of the town's music
you can barely hear the songs
you know by heart. Go back,

you will have to. Someone sits inside the night for you.
You could fall away with her
by your bed, singing carefully to your closing sleep.

The Fields of the Country

Since morning you've been on the tennis court,
playing against the backboard
at the far field of the plot,
near the end of the acreage. Your husband
has invited guests who want you to stop;
"Honey, you're no machine. Come up
and have a drink with us."
They can't hear you answer.

After lunch I am served large strawberries
which I eat without slicing.

Legs crossed, I sit under your sunhat
like a small queen. My brown hair lightens
moving with the breeze
and I feel very young.
No one sees me watching you
continue to play tennis with the wall.

It rains. Alone on the porch
I look for you in the telescope
but everything is a bit off.
I find the face of a small dog
who is lying still in the tomato field
among the other sickly dogs.
Nose against the glass
he looks up at me like the last hope.
I put out my hand for all of them
but they don't see it.

Throughout the house people are shouting;
"You'll really get sick now. Come inside."
Then the tennis balls fall dead with rain.
I put you in a towel and you whisper,
"Nothing is right. Please help me."
There are faces in the windows
mouthing and waving furiously to bring you in.

But I want to take you
to visit the observatory hidden among the wild berries.
We can go on the astronomer's tour
and set our eyes up against the larger lens.
The great dome will split
and stars will pour down
our open throats like tonic.
That is the dream. Here,
I'm walking with you down the hill
to the den of moaning dogs.

AHMOS ZU–BOLTON

Blackjack Moses

Being a preacher, he
would address himself to the spirit.
He voiced it all over
in the ghetto, churches
city council meeting
at the last turn
in the alley.

We caught his act in Baton Rouge.
He was chanting to a college group
had them repeating riddles:
nigger-om.
nigger-om.

We considered him foolish
& talked about him allnight.
Wrote all our friends
about his show, told them
to catch a g-movie
when he came to town.

Last we heard
he was jiving to a crowd of thousands.

the governor of ollie street

1

he was the only one of us
to be on time. for sunday school,
for band practice, for the gangmeetings

in the alley.

all this sat him right with the oldfolk
& we never elected him to anything
because of it.

but he was our leader as surely
as he was his father's son.

(his father:
a hellraising preacher
of the old school:
bringing the wrath of the lawd almighty upon us
if we didn't change our niggerways.

2

ollie street is 2 blocks long
with a dead-end both ways.
our nation. where
home was.

until we realized
that we were growing up
we would have defended our nation
against all.

love is a dead-end he told us
but it looks like we gotta choose it
anyhow.

3

so in the 8th grade we put sapphire
on his virgin tail. *love? love
nigger? here some love,*
we screamed.

Thru Blue Eyes

From the Diary of Livewire Davis

(if i looked into a mirror
thru blue eyes, i would fear
that reflection.
                    it would be deformed
after centuries of being gangleader
in a world of tribes.

i would have to crack
that reflection, to see if a darkness
would shine thru.

if i turn away from that mirror
with my vision still blued & blurred,
catch me on the stage in city park
lecturing on the fall of my father's home.
only i will invent it as i go along,
create it
            from the top of my
marijuana high.

i could never smash
that mirror. i could never
crash thru my eyes
to other-worlds

so completely
that i would not ever remember
that reflection.

RODGER KAMENETZ

Biograph

Better to be a crow, they said
and whip through thickets
or perch high atop a pine
and caw death down
to a fat hiker in shorts

And crows are glorious
with black jagged wings
flashing yellow corn
in their beaks
taking long mellow flights
and never dying in public

but to drift over cities
princely and unemployed
watching clouds buckle
sloughing their preserves
like great sloppy pies—

And the food—
sea bass, striped and musky
chubbies, dark and roiling—
clams—dropped from heights
or the bait some fisherman left
drying on the dock

but I am thin
for mostly I lack
the tact to stop
At night, the wind unbuttons me
I huddle with my wings
closed about my craw

Christopher Magisto

I work in a theater
where the magic tricks
go too slowly for the audience
until they weep or cry out

Always fooled
by their desire to know everything
they are as cruel as they are conscious
When they ask for the trick
I empty my sleeves

They close their eyes
and give me their dreams
which I turn into objects
that tumble down long shafts
In the bright sunlight
they disappear

The house lights come on
bringing deep clarity and regret
The audience has aged
Old women leave the places of young mothers
Their children have become men

They no longer care
how I do it

T.R. JAHNS

Utility

Here is the old one we can still use.
Quiet and cushioned, he merits
the corner. Prop up his legs
where he lies to balance saucers on
till the cup's half-full.
Spilled on, he won't spot or complain.

His blubbered stomach will make
a fine footstool.
When we stomp in out of the rain
we'll clean the mud from our boots
in his thin hair, knocking
the big chunks off with his elbow.
We'll toss our hats on his gnarled feet
when we come home from work,

it's neater.
He's useful, I tell you.
He won't get in the way.
Not like he did years ago when he
demanded we call him
Father.

RYAH TUMARKIN GOODMAN

Silence Spoke With Your Voice

Silence spoke with your voice
As you slept.
Silence kept
Your singing voice
Locked in the cell of sleep.
Yet when you woke,
Your orchard voice
Was warm as summer seas,
And silence, cold as a crow
On the bough of night,
Perched on your spray of speech.

Portrait

On a highly polished table
A portrait of my father and mother.
They have come to stay.
They never leave.
The stern look never changes,
The soft look never changes.

They watch me change,
Say nothing.
I speak to their silence,
They listen.

What are they thinking,
Standing so close to each other?
That they are young,
Younger than I?

I have not yet been born,

But they know me by heart,
Celebrate my birthdays,
Hold my eyes in their eyes.

Trapping time under glass,
The dead never age,
Never die.

What was flesh
Is still flesh.
Hands are still warm
In caracul muffs.
Love still unspoken.
Under their lids
So many tears unwept.

I forgive them their death.
They forgive me my life.

Ancestors

I am heavy with ancestors:
Headstones on my head,
Epitaphs in my eyes
That no one reads,
Dead fingers
Strumming on my heart.

I am heavy with origins:
Roots deepening,
Digging into me
As into a grave.

This weight I wear lightly,
But the weight of the unborn
Buries me.

The Business of Living

I am getting out of the business of living
To become a merchant of dust.
Selling buckets, barrels of dust.
My only rival is the wind
Blowing my profits.

Some manufacture loneliness,
I manufacture dust
Nesting on leaves, branches,
Sidewalks, sills;
Darkening mirrors.

My business is booming;
I need more space.
I move my merchandise
To the cemetery,
Make partners of the dead.

MICHAEL BERRYHILL

Rhetoric

With it, Plato thought poets might rule the world.
Something's gone awry. Throw it overboard
poets say. We'll have nothing left but the word
shining, a thing itself. Sunlight will simply shine
through that window. A black dog on a gold carpet
will merely bite itself or a passing fly. Things
will be as they are; irony being passé—a straightarm
against the hard tackle of pure sensation, the blues
an exaggeration. Even the caterpillar
puts us on. We will go from one thing
to the next; that man, a thrust, that woman
a suction of flesh. When it's all over and our
relations assemble, we will roll up our eyeballs
like windowshades and say, "Take my pain, take
my dying; words can't protect you now."

For Borges

Peron is back and wants to make you chicken inspector.
Governments never prized efficiency anyway. Frankly,
I don't trust you myself. You would tell me I died years age
On a flatboat on the Missouri River pursuing Manifest Destir
Sometimes a man with a knife attacks me in my dreams,
But we don't have a laugh over a drink later.

When my poems appeared opposite your story, I thought
They would be sucked into it, vanish from the page.
Often I confirm their identity—I will not say reality—
Always they are there. I write this over tea
And the thoughts of absent women.

You are on Columbus's map—at the edge of the world.
While the sand still trickles through the hourglass,
You wonder whether to turn it over again. Conventionally
It is the ideal shape of woman. That suffices.
The smell of coffee is more than Pope's remedy
For headache. It is the final icon.
Someone reads to you from *Treasure Island*, a cartographer's
Dream. I am hiding in the apple barrel.

KATHA POLLITT

A Turkish Story

The rugweaver kept his daughters at home, unmarried.
The soft clash of their bangles said *wish for us, wish.*

Longing for a son, a handsome agronomist,
for years he worked on a rug that would have no errors:

the blue was disappointment, the red was rancor.
His daughters circled their eyes with kohl and went
to the market,

they stirred pots, singing
a song about a lion asleep under an almond tree.

When he died each married a husband strong as the sea.
They danced on the rug, and its errors blazed like stars.

Blue Window

That longing you have to be invisible,
transparent as glass, thin air—
that is what moves you certain times to tears
watching the evening fill with city lights
and the long dusty summer avenues
rise weightless through the air
and tremble like constellations in a sky
so deep and clear you are your one desire,
Oh, let me be that blue. . . .

It is your other, solitary self
that calls you to the window where you stand
dreaming in the dusk in an ecstasy of longing
while your white apartment full of plants and pictures

grows strange with shadows, as though underwater.
And in another moment
you would stream out the window and into the sky like a breath—
but it is almost too dark to see. In the next apartment
a door is flung open. Someone speaks someone's name.

In Horse Latitudes

What does the sea want, my clothes, my keys, my face?
This is the mind's Sargasso,
expansive as Kansas flatlands, the big dead place.

The weeds stir, they make promises. I'm light as a shell.
Immobile, the sea bottom
glints at my emptiness with ship's tackle, jewels,

railway tickets, photographs: the blue-eyed platoons
grinning up from their doomed jungles.
I am left with nothing to hold, nothing to do

but imagine those horses the Spaniards abandoned here:
at night I have seen them rise
to graze the glassy prairie and whinny their fear.

Anxious, disconsolate,
they sniff for a wind. Sour water drips down their tails.
Ghost horses, I am like you: when the gray line of a sail

threads the horizon, my heart strains forward too:
heavy with salt, the blood
leans like a tide, but has no place to go.

The Horse Latitudes are a region of unusual calm in the North
Atlantic Ocean. When sailing ships were becalmed there, cargo
and horses would be thrown overboard. Thus lightened, the ship
could take advantage of whatever wind there might be.

245

KIRTLAND SNYDER

the white shark:
notes for a history

-in loving memory of my father

God tried to teach Crow how to talk.
Love, said God. Say, Love.
Crow gaped, and the white shark crashed into the sea
And went rolling downwards, discovering its own depth.

-"Crow's First Lesson"
Crow, by Ted Hughes

The shores are patrolled by sharks,
eastcoast and west alike.
Don't look, they're there all right,
and it's better not to see them
as you dunk yourself.

-"Sharks"
Variety Photoplays, by Edward Field

Guide to Kulchur: a mousing round for a word, for a
shape, for an order, for a meaning, and last of all for
a philosophy. The turn came with Bunting's line:

Man is not an end-product,
Maggot asserts.

The struggle was, and still might be, to preserve
some of the values that make life worth living.
And they are still mousing around for a significance
in the chaos.

-from the Foreword to
Guide to Kulchur, by Ezra Pound

prologue

first there was nothing
into which God stepped
as into animal dirt
in the gutter.

God wiped with disgust
the dirt from his foot
and made Crow
with blackness and feathers
and a horrible stink
and cry.

next came love
which was nothing more
than a word.
God could pronounce it
but it meant nothing
in the silence
so God turned to Crow.

out of the impossibility of love
came the white shark
whose natural course
was downward
to the slime
at the bottom of the sea

that was creeping steadily
towards the shores.

the white shark followed it.

his submission was called culture
and history.

1.

the shark is an unsubtle destroyer
lifting his white jaws
like a blizzard
in which all but the sheltered
are lost.

the white shark ravages the sea
like a barbarian
in a cathedral.

keen as a businessman
the white shark loves his work.

the white shark flies his fin
like a flag.

the fin splicing the water
is a signal of destruction,

a fleet of fins
is a holocaust

or a business deal worth millions.

the sheltered spend their time
watching the small fish
freeze in the white shark's jaws;

later they will eat the remaining bones.

2.

the white shark possesses a briefcase

in which he carries a copy
of *Moby Dick*
that he has read
and wished he were a whale
or a conglomerate
or a corporation

instead of a single killer.

3.

the white shark loves the Gulf Stream
and the Florida Peninsula
and the Presidential Mansion
to which he has often been invited.

the white shark waits
for Fidel to take a swim.

4.

the white shark smiled
at the news of Neruda's death,

and wasn't far from Guernica
when Franco smiled

nor from Chile
when the murdered Allende
was thrown to the dogs.

the white shark plays tennis in South Africa.

the white shark watched
the Portuguese Army

tear open the bellies of pregnant women
and bayonet the fetuses
like olives at cocktail hour.

the white shark sailed to Vietnam
which almost aged him
his joy was so complete.

5.

the white shark swims in the Harlem River
and in the uptown Hudson
keeping an eye on the poor
whose color is an enemy.

the white shark swims in the Mississippi
waiting for Nigger Jim
to fall overboard.

the white shark was in the Ohio
caressing himself
like a sperm whale
over the deaths at Kent State.

the white shark had a wet dream
about a black shark
as the Jackson State Massacre
climaxed on national television.

6.

the white shark was what Narcissus saw
in the pool.

the white shark was the last thing
Hart Crane struck
in the Caribbean.

the white shark swims in the attics
of the suburban houses.

the white shark covered the earth with water
so that it would be his.

7.

in God's image
was the white shark created:
blind, white, and deadly.

the white shark cannot fathom
his existence
nor does he care to
in the murky depths.

the white shark prefers blood
for its lack of subtlety
and inflammatory hue.

the smell of blood in the water
comes to the white shark
like a formal invitation
from a head of state.

the white shark is a blunt instrument
looking for the crania
of good men.

8.

the white shark is afraid of the dark
and of undesignated places
and of incomprehensible people and objects

and his fear of these conditions
worsens if they continue to exist

until it demands someone's death

or the destruction of something mysteriously beautiful

or the illumination of some impenetrable darkness
that will not yield to the light.

9.

i have seen the white shark
swallow the children of the poor
and vomit up the children of the sheltered rich
in their crisp playclothes.

i have seen the white shark's
insatiable teeth
tear open honest men
like business envelopes.

i have seen the white shark
tumbling delightfully
in the glare of Hiroshima,

deriding the laments
of the dying.

i have seen him steer nations
into chaos and death
where even politicians
could not make sense
of the carnage.

i have seen him clerically
blessing death,

keeping silent
when the sin was so mortal

it demanded outrage

image of the history

dunked and floating
on the sea,
bleeding invisibly
to the cruising sharks

we read editorials
on our backs
even as the white shark
sniffs us for his meals.

cabanas gleam like rainbows on the beaches

growing like brown vines in the sand

shoots of barbed wire
curl out of one war into another.

issuing like maggots
the sheltered appear on the shores

waving like allies to the circling fins.

the water trembles and disturbs us slightly.

the white shark lifts his jaws.

sharkflesh gleams like a blizzard, like emptiness.

we come eye to eye at last
with the whiteshark's godless vision.

later the sheltered eat our remaining bones.

WILLIAM HEATH

Haystack Calhoun
for Toby Olson

i have seen the turnbuckles shudder
and explode—
the force of his head.

i have seen the mat become quicksand
heard the splintering
outscream the crowd
as the floor boards
refuse to hold.

the huge man standing, unsmiling,
the mat flared up and out about him,
his eyes, for once, level with the bottom rope;
the man standing like the loaded
stamen of some monstrous
poison flower,
while the queen bees buzzed.

but given his weight:
one foot on each scale
each scale whipping to 300, the limit,
holding erect there an instant, before
the glass snaps.

a farmboy so dumb
he threw his big chance:
the coach's car, the fierce animal
decaled on the door,
the car panting in the ditch—
that stench of burnt rubber.

what other kind of a man

would wreck a car like that,
run through corn, to ask a boy
giant with a plow
to point toward town?
the boy so dumb he didn't know
though he scratched his head hard
with the plow
till the blood flowed with his sweat—
the coach, eyes up, aghast, walked
backward to his car.

no ring could hold
the boy-man in his rage.
what man could last
against him?

i have seen him breach upwards
like a whale, the flying
scissors hold, his legs,
the whale's jaw, bite
the neck
leaving another near dead Jonah
beached on the mat.

yet some have survived
this hold—
the loss of their ears,
have regained feet
only to be trampled by an elephant
flung from the sling
of the ropes.

hang on for this fat man
has a final notorious hold:
this one he ricochets around the ring
like a pin-ball machine gone berserk,
he side-swipes his man
to the mat, recoils
from the ropes, flings himself up into the air

and dives,
belly-crashing his victim,
flopping on him like a blubber landslide,
a tidal wave of flesh.

some men have lived
to smother in this hold:
"The Big Splash."

HEATHER McHUGH

Wheels

However much the highway makers want
to redesign it, land
is not rectangular, and birds resist
the shortest distances between two points
of rest. Even the interstate
must make concessions, breasted
by hills, bushwhacked by whatever
stubborn undergrowths of hair.
Tacked on a wall, America's at home,
the state lines stack up square
against the rectitude of architects.
But travellers find in fact,
by accident, by air,
in window cinemas of stream
and film and field no understated
frames: the inland borderlines
are lost in their translation, are
not there. And all the mapmen, Mad-
ison Avenue small talk and model
mongers stay unmoved by dust
and thunder storms, becoming
more remote to me, who hit
the road, than any ruminant
well-meaning cows that don't
know one tit from another.
Down to earth, I know her
shifting motherhood, I leave
a little rubber on her lips. The tourist
pictures tell the truth: the earth
is very old. Her lovers learn
no ease or symmetry on trips.
My roadmap, full of wrinkles,
will not fold.

YWCA

Ex-Christian and sex-lover, what
am I doing here? Husbandless,
quarterless, too suddenly
consigned to frugality's room
at the top, a room that looks out
on the cityscape I've missed these many
years—a strict, unpopulated
zone of slopes and tile. Inside,
the sad-designer-style
of singlemindedness: one
chair, one desk, one dresser, one
one-body bed. No evidence of a loving
past, mess of relations, father
and son. Breaking rules, I break out
my rye bottle. Soon the room turns gold.
The window's inch of air admits
a mile of secular six-o'clock chanting,
traffic. So the two-man god has gone
off-duty, so the habit's been abandoned, so
what? Here the sun is setting
its aloof example: burned, but powerful,
a fat red balancing act on the blackest
edge of hours or a roof. Let me learn
it now, lord, one
can be enough.

TOM O'GRADY

The Old Ladies

I have found paper
with their markings, bills
stuffed in shoes to keep
the satin toes pointed
and regular like a row
of gleaming fish, and pieces
of dolls wrapped in string
for hanging things. In
one box alone I discovered
their voices white and creaking
and imagined them staring
out of windows, searching
for the right word. At the end
of the garden a mound of bottles
catches light and I spend all
afternoon searching for dates.
The old ladies have heen here,
moving in and out like a wind.
There are some old pictures bent
to keep a window tight or stop
a door which we straighten in
the light to catch a face or
match a dress with them before
they were old—In the evening
I hunt inside, opening and closing
letters for a scent, sit quiet
in the old bedroom tracing
a sun's shadow, tuning my breath
to their breathing when it comes
like the cautious deer at the edges
of our black field.

Living in Another Man's House

I expect you're planted somewhere
in the tangled pine coming apart
still after all this time, like
the legends of war treasures fast
in the land and the ribbons of
bodies left to harden the clay.
My neighbor says the land is rich;
his animals scream when they see
him, his calves fatten themselves
on roadgrass, their necks pressing
the barbed-wire of his place.
And I imagine you assert the past
somewhere, fondling trinkets of
memory like smooth stones. I was
told there were murders here, that
all you began finished with sons
leaping breathless to war, and you
read about their lives in newspapers.
Now this slumbering house leans in
the thick breeze up from the streams,
small amid trees you started, and
I enter its echoes head down, wondering
who first loved on these floorboards
and who carried their solitude
up the stairs.

VIRGINIA R. TERRIS

Husbands

You flee their igloos
and toil over Arctic tundras.
Your shadows have short fat legs even at noon.
The blubber you eat ruins your digestion.
Oh, why were you ever born north of the Arctic Circle?

So you go to Africa.
The fruit is golden.
Your digestion improves. But
in your dreams you return to the ice shelf.
You say Hello. You drop your bad feelings
down the ice holes where you catch seals
to feed your children.

You forget you have a way of walking
that makes warm citizens edgy.
Sometimes you slip into polar language.
Sometimes your lashes are frosty.

But they are waiting for you. As your tongues
freeze to your palates
the agitation of chilly fires welcomes you home,
the sinking back into the Arctic night.

Tracking

I learned one kind of thing in the house
the woman thing. Mother
taught me the woman thing.
How to make bread that was warm.
How to sew with a warm needle.
How to dust warm furniture.

I was a warm girl in a warm house.

And other things in the shop out back.
Father taught me to carpenter.
Run a metal lathe. Solder.
While he poured cement, I put on swords.
I hit a bull's-eye with a .22.
I was as brave as he was strong.

But once alone in the hills at dusk
skirting the woods, the house
a window glowing far away,
I saw in the blue snow, interrupting me,
fresh tracks of a panther hunting meat.
I never told them about the tracks
home where they were and I
on a long fearful trek
across a winter's night.

The Stink of Burning Egg

The stink of burning egg in my nose,
I write you a letter.
Although I have been writing how I love you
I am reminded of another matter—
how I hate you.

Your eggs.
Why do I think of them now?
I've never seen just one and never
in a pot charred.

But explosions?
My hand trembles on the handle
as I run cold water over them.

Shall I turn off the stove?

Save the pot?
Let the whole thing explode?

I'll mail you my letter in the shell
and let the P.O.
put the whole thing together.

Stigmata

The palm of my hand bleeds.
I can't remember why.
But I remember the saints.

As I look at that round red spot
in the center I ask
if I must always suffer. I ask
if I must dedicate my life. I ask
if I must sacrifice my life.

And then I ask
if I must hide my hand
so no one
will fall down before me.

Whoever You Are

Whoever you are who took my porte-feuille
don't think you've dug a piece out of me.
I'm not bleeding.

You're only part of the landscape.
I've always known there were thieves.
I've been stolen from before and
I've gone on living—more terrible things—
and I've known the thief—and loved him

and we've never agreed on reparations.

What you've taken is already
wine, piss, a wet spot on a wall.

It hurts most because I don't know
who you are. And I didn't know
you were taking it.

I'm angry because you deprived me
of looking at you and making believe
nothing was happening.

A Walk With My Cat

The wind closes the door behind us.

We sit sniffing on the porch.
At first my nose won't work.
I watch her head shifting.
I watch how the scent goes in.
Then I find the tomcat upwind.

We go down the stairs
one foot on one step,
slow without hurrying, to the bottom ground
the stones, the thawing grass cold on our feet.

A bird sits on the fence.
We crouch. We rush.
The bird flies off.

I forget the birds I have loved.
The eyes of my cat
point to a lapsed wing.
I forget the pain of the scent of dying.
Blood dyes my lips.

The breastbone yields.

We search for soft clean earth
scratch open the hole and squat.
It is good to shit under the sky
under the March clouds.

We avoid shadows.
We roll on the warm bricks.
Stretching our bellies to the sun
our paws open.
Wind runs across us.

Our eyes fall together.
We nod with our noses rubbing against the ground.

As we drowse in the sun
I do not know what to call my cat.

There are no words for us.

Being on the Edge of Someone Else

your center, the membrane of your center
rupturing
   and your fluids
flowing out generously
     but partly unwilling
into
  the unsettling fluids of another
not amorous but intense and haunting
either the other
    or yourself
    opening yourself
to another's hurt

you continue to be outside

with a broken skin
so the other's slight tremor
shudders through you
you end it by
                denying it
        or losing it
or killing it

you can say
                It is not mine but another's
    or
                Who is that other?

KEITH ALTHAUS

Poem

Begin here; where I began.
Across the yard, over unmarked graves
of starlings and goldfish, this house
casts the same shadow that fell
inside me twenty years ago, darkened
nerves and left them stained. Enter
where new paint on the door jamb
hides ruler marks and dates under its skin.
Come down green stairs and ladders
to my childhood; in the rushing dark
watch secrets cross like beams of light
and shine along the bones, hunting faces
at windows in the blood. Cross
the cold calendar of memory, the scar tissue
in the mind's picturing flesh. Touch
my beginning and leave; rise
out of coal cellars lined with canning jars,
past rooms of upset games, into my arms
around this house the night we met.

In the Hammersmith Public Library
for Lois

It's all here:
the spoils,
the sacked cities, skulls
piled to the sun, blood
dried to ink.
Who was it said he saw
the print flying off the page
like flocks of tiny birds?
I forget. I should go;

book by book I only
balance my forgetting.
I should go and leave it
to these muttering old men who
are just pretending to read.
Shakespeare for a pair of shoes?
Or the other way around —
Librarians are more important
than libraries. Living print!
A book you can take to bed,
read in the dark. We need
a reference for the hand, the breast,
the hair; our illiterate flesh.

Indian Summer Garden Party

False places, air flowers, spines,
showers of spears in the ice cubes
melting on the lawn. What does the grass think?
That it's hail? That summer is over?
It is. This is a mirage.
Looking at birds, thinking they're bats,
in a staggering flight in the top
of the pines, everything outlined
in black. The last of the coffee! Rides home!
Dresses passing under the hemlock
so white and blank nothing can be written on them.

Traveling in Europe
for my younger brother

Half a century of smoke, burned
lifeless air, has stained the windows
of this dome improbable colors —
violet-grays, white-browns and greens,
the colors of pigeons. I listen

to the slow waltz of canes
across the platform and row on row
of steel lockers rattling in the wake
of the last express as I wait for the last
train from the Zoo Station, across
from the zoo, where I heard that afternoon
the tap-tap of a lemur's claws
as it paced to exhaustion, a fast heart
in the stale air of the house
for small carnivores.
Wiping my hands in my pockets
I wad balls of lint with sweat,
finger the edge of a folded map,
the schedule, and my ticket—
safe, in a lump of crumbs
and coins that are useless now;
I thumb them like a blind man
and tell their value—
have I been here that long?

Tomorrow's paper, cigarettes,
a package of biscuits
for this night journey back
the other set of rails,
the cities in reverse,
the distances undone
but not the time.
Traveling at night
there's nothing to see
but myself in the black window,
the darkness pressing through
my pores and the occasional lights
of cities in the distance
passing behind my forehead

Half asleep: the station lights running through
the compartment are the headlights of cars
crossing the ceiling of that room
where rabbits fought on the wall beside my bed—

how could I lose? one hand against the other:
which one should I let win? —
Nights we lay awake, talking
in low voices across the dark.
We asked each other why it couldn't be
that all of this, the whole world,
was just an atom, a speck of dust
in another world, and that world
only a speck of dust in a bigger world;
on and on our talk spiraled in the dark,
infinity in all directions! until
our voices dropped off and our thoughts slowed
with our breaths and we fell asleep.

My head in a bundled coat
against the jolting wall;
you envy me I think,
uncomfortable in your comfort,
pangs and twinges but never
the full-blown pain that blows a life apart, don't:
be happy there tonight stuck to her with sweat,
for nothing really holds us anywhere,
least of all inside, where the strings
keep tangling and the journeys end
in knots. From that room I left first,
here, nowhere, tonight
I've thought for you, for all of us,
traveling at night, holding in the dark
what remains of wonder.

Middle River

Birds' mirror and host
to these crabbers and pleasure boats
that shuttle in and out of the marina
while we idle for fuel and shade
our eyes to watch the jets

from Martin-Marietta strafe
the Chesapeake. The water
is calm, safe, reflecting
the contrails breaking up
and the new moon dissolving
like a pill in the brackish inlet
until a speedboat interrupts
the picture, drawing shouts
from fishermen along the shore
as it cuts across their lines,
scaring any fish, leaving
in its wake, undisturbed
below, the blood worms
bleeding to death in the current,
losing all shape but the hook.

The Somnambulist Blue

The somnambulist blue, narcotic sky
of early evening, when over the roofs
and wires and branches appear. . .
like something obvious suddenly remembered,
or seen, as in a picture that can be
looked at two ways, a puzzle drawing
from The Children's Page, whose gardens
and woods, spaces in thickets and trees,
endlessly hide faces; mouths formed
by a vine, eyes and hair made out of leaves
and sky; so now, suddenly seen as always
there. . . appear, in the beginning of the night
above me, *the stars,* beautiful as questions:
where is your hand? are you asleep?

BINNIE KLEIN

Next Time We Meet

Next time we meet let's
keep our clothes on
okay? and
I'll caress your
high school memories
touch gently
all your ambitions
release my tongue
onto your talent
cup my hand around
the hard, small
surface of your
favorite thoughts
kiss deep into
the times you've
had fever and
your dreams were
knotted up and hot
you'll stroke
my hairy madness
and rub your talent
against my imagined
poetry reviews

oh your touch is so glossy
let's skim over
our pages all night

HERBERT KROHN

My Flute

When I had learned enough to fail every test
I began to play a flute called "blueman's rainbow"
color of the third rail
engines keep kissing
to make them strong and travel.
My flute called "enemy of silence"
frees every prisoner
in the midnight special hour
when silver chimes with the silver
moon quarter
of a million miles away.
Nothing inside my flute then
measures the nothing that keeps us apart.
My flute called "what is your real name?"
says no to rhetorical questions.
Three joints it has like a finger
point to an open door
but me and my flute called "second nature now"
stay in the empty window the world goes by.

Two Vietnamese Women

Do you have "my wife" in States?
How long you stay Saigon?
Maybe ti-ti, maybe beaucoup.
I like you too much.
And I no say I *love* you too much!
Next time you come to *New York Bar*
I love you too much.
Hey, you buy me Saigon Tea?

My Darling,

yesterday evening was too hot.
I called the wind
then, ti-ti, I fall asleep.
Maybe midnight,
maybe midnight I wake up.
I write to you this letter
by many small candle
then I cry many sweat.
You see where they fall
on my letter?
Maybe after one year you go back States—
no sweat.
Maybe V.C. fini you—
I be too sad.

HARRY STESSEL

Speech for an Abdication

In W.W. II the Japanese
negotiators' car
ran out of gas
en route to the surrender

while that officer in Petrograd
wishing to decree martial law
could not find any paste
to go behind his posters

and on the day the crowd
cracked the Bastille with fingers
and stones, Louis wrote
in his daybook, *Nothing.*

I bring these instances
together, not as samples
of history's heavy humor
nor in arrogant belief

that I might have
outgoverned the
wretchedest of Romanovs
but in consolation for

kingdoms fumbled like
balls through baby fingers
rolling down every slope
loving the middle of the world.

Iowa

After Boris slays the tsarevitch Dmitri
the "false Dmitri"
shows up in Poland
raises an army, marches on Russia
reigns for a hundred days
is shredded
the shreds wadded into a cannon
and shot back to Poland
like Quaker Oats.
Shortly a second, falser Dmitri
re-appears in Poland.
He claims to have survived.

    Poland is like Iowa
    snowy, flat and normal
    no picturesque injustices
    no crystal orb, no Czar.

When the Czar captures
10,000 Moravians
he blinds ninety-nine of every hundred
docking the hundredth of only one eye
to lead his cohorts
home through Poland
unsightly lesson to their masters.

    But in Iowa
    the newsboy knocks and not the news.
    A cannister collects for the blind
    not a hundred cardboard heads
    slotted with a single eye.

When the Czarina's lover
plays the snowy fields
she architects
a palace of ice on the Neva
icy beds and mirrors

blinis and wines
coverlets and sheets of ice
and weds him to a Kalmuk dwarf, a hunchback
nude in January:
after the wedding night, pneumonia.

I live in Poland—
that is, Iowa—with my wife
Anastasia
(between us is no
Russian winter
but immaculate fidelity
mutual goals)
but when the snow
east to Vladivostok
is unbroken by a hundred tracks
and rime, indiscriminate
granulates on every twig
nostalgic to begin my reign
I claim to have survived
and lift an orb of snow.

A Charm Against Pregnancy

We wait for the
serendipity of blood,
haunted by
white wicker carriages
and cribs, by
babyclothes of
milkshake colors.

Sideways to the mirror
she reads her pouch
for occupancy.
Into her rich
Egyptian court has

a tiny Moses come?
Is my plum
about to have a pit?
Are her tits more
sensitive,
is she tireder, more
queasy in the morning than is usual?

"Why don't you pray to
a Jewish saint?"
No one occurs to me
but Billy Rose.
St. Billy, send us
blood, a testament
to insulation.
Please, God, blood. I
promise to buy only
Trappist jelly.

Please let blood
mark the door to
her womb, that the Angel
of Life may pass by.

ROSS TALARICO

The Balancing

Once again the best foot
Has gone forward.
But the other still lingers
In its grave.
I had some plans,
Some laughs, and now

My eyeglasses go on reading
All by themselves.
Someone's finger keeps moving
Along the map
Of the body's inland; my rivers
Shift, some roads need paving,
The deer are finally crossing.

The moon rises again;
It is a ball of yarn a woman
Knits a sweater from.
Will she place it
Over the dark shoulders I bring
To her sleep? In a dream
I am walking silently
Across a trampoline.

My eyes steady themselves.
What horizon are they expecting
This time? Daylight is a full page
Of advertising.
I stare into it, and finally
Beyond it. In the distance
A stillness carries the silence
Of an understanding: how long
The teeter-totter has waited
For the identical twins
That sit upon it.

ELLEN BRYANT VOIGT

Tropics

In the still morning when you move
toward me in sleep for love,
I dream of

an island where long-stemmed cranes,
serious weather vanes,
turn slowly on one

foot. There the dragonfly folds
his mica wings and rides
the tall reed

close as a handle. The hippo yawns,
nods to thick pythons,
slack and drowsy, who droop down

like untied sashes
from the trees. The brash
hyenas do not cackle

and run but lie with their paws
on their heads like dogs.
The lazy crow's caw

falls like a sigh. In the field
below, the fat moles build
their dull passage with an old

instinct that needs
no light or waking; its slow beat
turns the hand in sleep

as we turn toward each other

in the ripe air of summer
before the change of weather,

before the heavy drop
of the apples.

Claiming Kin

Insistent as a whistle, her voice up
the stairs pried open the blanket's
tight lid and piped me
down to the pressure cooker's steam and rattle.
In my mother's kitchen, the hot iron
spit on signal, the vacuum
cleaner whined and snuffled.
Bright face and a snazzy apron,
clicking her long spoons,
how she commandeered the razzle-dazzle!

In the front room I dabbed
the company chairs with a sullen rag
(Father's drawers—nothing
wasted). Pale lump blinking
at the light, I could hear her sing
in her shiny kingdom: the sound
drifted out like a bottled message.
It was the voice of a young girl,
who stopped to gather cool moss, forgetting
the errand, spilling the cornmeal,
and cried and cried in her bearish papa's ear.

At night, while I flopped
like a fish on grandma's spool bed,
up from her bed and my wheezing
father she rose to the holly,
flat-leaf and Virginia Creeper.
Soft ghost, plush as a pillow,

she wove and fruited against the black hours:
red berries and running cedar, green signatures
on the table, on the mantle.

Mother, this poem is from your middle
child who, like your private second self,
rising at night to wander the dark house,
grew in the shady places:
a green plant in a brass pot,
rootbound, without blossoms.

Farm Wife

Dark as the spring river, the earth
opens each damp row as the farmer
swings the far side of the field.
The blackbirds flash their red
wing patches and wheel in his wake,
down to the black dirt; the windmill
grinds in its chain rig and tower.

In the kitchen, his wife is baking.
She stands in the door in her long white
gloves of flour. She cocks her head and
tries to remember, turns like the moon
toward the sea-black field. Her belly
is rising, her apron fills like a sail.
She is gliding now, the windmill churns
beneath her, she passes the farmer,
the fine map of the furrows.
The neighbors point to the bone-white
spot in the sky.

Let her float
like a fat gull that swoops and circles,
before her husband comes in for supper,
before her children grow up and leave her,

before the pulley cranks her down
the dark shaft, and the church blesses
her stone bed, and the earth seals
its black mouth like a scar.

RONALD WALLACE

One Hook

I knew it was too late
when these blue fish
moved cooly out of the painting.
Klee, I said, what is happening?
What do we do?
But he was fishing, madly fishing.
Make hooks, he said.

Some of the fish slipped smoothly
into the cunts of little girls.
Some hung ties around their necks
and worked for I.B.M.
Some raised hard fins
and swam on highways,
fish-mouths honking like horns.

And everything they touched turned
to fish.
The stars wore slime.
The moon grew gills.
Trees darted quickly away
in schools.
They ate the grass, the weeds,
the people like kelp
and laid their eggs.

Klee, Klee! I said,
what is happening?
What do we do?
But he was fishing, madly fishing.
Make hooks, he said.

RON H. BAYES

The Casketmaker

Because it pleases me I turn to you
this lightless hour, and ask a reassurance
that cannot be there, although you touch me
and respect a smile of which I'm half ashamed.

The time is mine and selfishly I share
the sudden flash, sheet lightning of my
mind, unapt to start a fire or cause a
rain, denote direction sure enough to take;

And you can see my clutching—like a sea
anemone poked with a stick, neither in defense
nor sure aggression out of will: I build,
I drive, I turn to you again. Admire the nail.

The Philadelphia Airport

Rather tired at the Philadelphia airport.
And the plane to board
an hour and three coffees away.

What irony that at five-thirty A.M.
I am at last moved by emotion
(it has been a long time) when
the unavoidable, continual soft-music loudspeaker
romps a certain German polka,

And I remember another airport,
other years,
and I who have never wished to go back before
wish to go back.

286

But one never can in time
(and does space matter much?).
Want some irony?
In Germany it was—you weren't there—
and I loved you: Christ! with what passion
of intensity; jealous of whomever you were with

With the dawn pink and blue and gray and
the trees mushroom clumping
like wanting Breughel
to red-in country rompers—or
maybe someone good at satyrs—

And I remember that other airport,
I remember a polka
and that I loved you.

Now each in maze muddled and adjusting
and we no longer love. Why kid? And I am not
even jealous in wild imaginings.

A few people,
a few more people:
now we move. . .you move. . .I move. . .from progress
to progress,
unlove to unlove,
anticipating only departures.

Rivage

a dark smoky room
with guitars and
french and german
and english words
broken; How do you say
kiss, *une bis,*
in german? They are all
german. In igloos they
sleep with a candle.
This is a flamingo song
about a mine
in Spain where the workers
work very hard.
It is sad.

and walking home
at three in the morning
the metro stops at 12:30
from the southern end
of Rue St. Jacques
to Gare de l'Est
by many side roads
got lost
and found myself
in St. Denis
the workingman's
whorehouse.

a girl who wore crosses
for earrings in a dark
smoky room near St. Denis
and a warm smile. She didn't
speak english, french, or german.

a dark smoky room
with guitars and
french and german
and english words
broken; How do you say
kiss, *une bis,*
in german? They are all
german. In igloos they
sleep with a candle.
This is a flamingo song
about a mine
in Spain where the workers
work very hard.
It is sad.

Ah, in Rivage,
he sings Dylan off key.
He is sad.
Every man needs protection
so Sisters of Mercy
have some sangria
and tell us how to say
kiss, *une bis.*

CYNTHIA MACDONALD

The Platform Builder

If you were to construct a platform,
    That is, if you wanted to construct a platform
  And then you did (after a lot of self-instruction
      On platform building and frequent consultation
  With the building supply people) and you worked
    Weekends till your friends, unobsessed with platforms,
    Stopped calling. And if, then, you finally got it built,
With what an invasion of accomplishment
                   you'd view it...the tools
Not even put away, but left beside the scaffolding,
  You'd buy three things you'd been wanting and
              thinking about buying
  And sit with an old friend to watch "The
            Shoeshine Boy" on TV
If it was on.

The next day, looking at your platform,
    You'd see the gap between the second and third planks
      And how the miters showed how many
  Times you had made corrections. If you made
Another platform, you'd fix those things. And in
            the thinking of another
    The need is there or maybe the need
    Made you think of it.
So you begin again. Of course, it is more difficult,
  Demanding a platform cantilevered on the first,
    A kind of step above a base.
You build it, with the foreseen result: like
            owners who correct
In every house they build the faults of the last one;
         the flaws are not
The same, but there are flaws.

With each successive platform, the skill increases
And the demands increase beyond the
                        increase of the skills;
The choice of wood, fitting without nails or glue, the curve
        To change direction at the sixteenth level
        When, emerging above the trees, it's evident
        The direction chosen affords a view
Of the oil storage tanks instead of the sea.
And then, a few levels higher, the question
                        whether wood at all
        Or plexiglass (acrophobia?) or steel (too cold in winter?),
Etc. And, on the twenty-second level, having
                        to stop completely
        For Zoning Board appeals because you've gone
Beyond the allowed height for an AA zone.
And interviews, and manufacturers who
                        want you to build
Another just the same, using their product.

Young builders, contemplating platforms,
        Examine what you've done and ask you how
You did those first ones and sometimes you say
                        you can't remember,
        Which is true, and sometimes you try
To think just how and answer with how you
                        did the latest ones
        Or even how you think you're going to do the next,
If you find time to do it.
And they imagine you content with, not so
                        much what you've made—
        They've heard of creative dissatisfaction—
But that it's been accepted; that you can
                        get money and more
Than money for a speech on "How I Build
                        Platforms" and only
        Will be asked to set another date
If you get drunk and don't show up.

291

If you want to build a platform, and ask for my advice,
        I'll give it, but remember
    I can't remember back to where you are...
    I think I would use wood to start,
    To get the platform's natural connection.
White ash is strong and tough and has escape built in its name.
        I think I cannot say it better than to say
If I were about to start to build a platform,
I think I'd start with ash.

A Story for a Child

The mushroom was beautiful.
Its pleats were as sharp and neat as
The folds of a half-closed silk fan.
Its skin was as smooth as the inside
Of a mouth. And it was resilient.
The gradations of tan to brown from
Edge to center were as subtle as those
On a color wheel, but had more depth.
Its setting of green moss and ferns was
Felicitous. It was fecund and dropped
Its spoors easily and freely. And
It was not aggressive. Its name,
Aminita Angelica was melodious.
All in all, the word for it was: perfection.
Unless what you wanted was an umbrella stand.

But it was more complicated than that if
What you were was a perfect mushroom yourself.
Consult *Snow White* for what would happen then. But
Remember that the happy ending was because
It was a story for a child.

Getting to the End

We are diagnosing the dream.
We have put it on the table,
Taken its pressures, measured its beats.

An exploratory is necessary.
We are anesthetizing the dream.
We are slitting its ripe belly.

We are performing an autopsy on the dream.
We have laid its organs out on the slab.
A perfect specimen.

We are reading the obituary of the dream.
It was widely beloved.
And celebrated.

We are visiting the grave of the dream.
Its tablet is bronze.
The lettering tells us what we already know.

The ribs of the dream close, caging our heads.
Our dreams are filled with the bones of desire.

The Stained Glass Woman

I

The reason I fall apart easily
Is because they have not discovered
What can hold me together. Lead works
In window junction points, but not in joints.
Other metals are too inflexible. Rubber stretches.
Clay crumbles. Plastics
Are cut by the motion of my glass anxiety.

II

You knew how to do it, or, rather, did it without completely
Knowing how; made the heart beat, turning blood from blue
To red; made the sections fuse, annealing them; made glass
Into skin. There are no purple or green edges to cut you when
You hold me. Now when I move, I move in unison with myself,
Through places transformed by my transformation.
Only sometimes when the weather changes, or I
                                      am tired or angry
Or walk into a church or see a Tiffany lamp, I ache where
The seams once were. Then I am afraid that if you leave me,
A glassy residue may spread through me as quickly
And quietly as the rising light flushes a rose window.

III

You are gone. You were only
The preparation for someone else.
I walk accompanying the prepared space.
My food and furniture are glass.
I look at a glass landscape
And hear glass music.
I protect myself
With the material of myself.
That woman with blood
Reddening the water in the tub
Is the one who can be cut.
I will carry glass flowers to her grave.

DALE MATTHEWS

Congress

The men wear wigs
like England but it's America.
I have to prove to them
that I am able
but I can't remember
what state I represent.

I am in a state of passion
a state of siege.
During recess
I kiss my lover's skin.
When the old men
call me in
I brush my hair
but I can't brush off this grin.

They bring me water.
They call a doctor.
They try to shield me
from the press
but the dress
slips off my shoulders.

I can't remember.
I yawn, I moan.
When the vote is called
I fall across my desk
and wake up dreaming
Alabama
Carolina
Iowa
Vermouth

This drunken lust disgusts them.
I turn my glass upside down
casting my vote for water.

The elder shakes me
trying to wake me.
I loll in his arms
like an ocean liner
rocking in dry harbor.

Small Favors

In a dream
the wall of green water
moved towards me,
arched itself in its own slow
time
miles
above shore
then froze:
a Chinese print.
Spray fanned out
like points of lace.

There was time to turn,
scramble from out its shadow
back to the village.
Lunch was being served
and sheets hung in the sun to dry
like so many
handkerchiefs.

Friend,
in a small world
small favors are possible.
My house would supply kindling
for a long winter but

now, a cup of coffee
before the sun moves another
inch in heaven.

The Dice Player

These dice in my hand
heavy as meteors.
All the constellations
have fallen before me,
little clusters of infinity
in this dark room.

Like the knuckles of lace-makers,
the purest cream they weave.
No. Stained
as the few teeth remaining
in the head of an old fool

But somehow perfect.
Not forms that pierce
or threaten to dissolve:
pencils, flowers, bits of meat. . .

Balanced as the workings of a clock
dice tumble in my dreams
through silent cylinders.
I pour it all,
have poured it all before me
as easy as water
from this cupped hand.

JORDAN SMITH

The Immigrant's Stars

The sky lowers, the angry weight
of Orion flattens the twilight against
the flat earth. I walk to town
west over land parcelled off for houses
in the spring, fields where ownership
spreads, frost between the farms
cramping the land small and hard as cash.
My coins slap face down on the bar,
sounds of ice splintering and the dead
rustle of cellophane on a cigarette pack,
the tearing in the stomach when a deed
switches hands. Harsh and sweet

as this whiskey I see the smooth grain
of your face, and your hair spilling
wheat through my hands. The old love
of fences and the long harvest rubs
rawly as new leather in my palms. Love,
when the snow falls from the hunter's belt
to repossess my land, when I see you
arched with a sickle moon over another man,
a knife's cold ache rises in my throat
and in my teeth a hate for whatever I have owned
or tried loving rings with the ice wind.

The gravity of my possessions
wears me down to a fist. I remember
nights when we drank on the warm roof
until the house and stars fell away as we held
together while the fields spun for miles.
Now I feel myself heavy and dedicated
to property, land poor as the farmers who sell
or go broke while suburbs rise with the taxes.

The radio gives tonight's storm a spread
of five counties; in all that land
there is no home, only the freedom
of being lost in the snow, of owning nothing.

All night I dream we are immigrants
in a country too vast for land surveys
or barbed wire. Your hair spreads
new fields across my shoulder, and the town
lifts, a strange constellation circling
upwards to its own season.

Blue River Falls

The minnows sheer out
from the falls. Their shadows
stretch thin and stone-dark
on the pool floor, shattering
where the sunlight breaks on the foam.
My eyes light with spray;
drops of sky and your hair wash
over my face in the curl and force
of this young current.
The colors pound. I lean
from you and the base rock swells
against my skin, a huge sadness
ancient and rising
dense enough to snap my back.
The fish shape of my tongue
floats still and dark
in the middle water, at its root
a fear of rock and depth,
of shining water the blue of your eyes.

SUSAN SNIVELY

An Afternoon with a Baby

Having no children, I am strange
to her. Her mother, when she is not
screaming, tells me I will have one
someday. She knows I would be good
at it. I am almost thirty. Not yet.

The little girl rocks & stares. I am
a queen or at least a godmother. She
wants to know if I shave my legs
& why I wear that funny stuff on my eyes. I talk
about my cats as if they were children.

Bathing in the big tub, she wants
the song about the fishes in the itty
bitty pool. I do not sing to her
because I feel motherly but because
I feel childish. Boop boop
diddum daddum waddum choo?

My daughter Shelley is inside my head. She
is not born yet
& maybe she never will be. No one
can tell me my future. Still
I miss her as if she had come & gone.

DAVID LEHMAN

Journey into the Eye

for Wesley Shrader

Having no choice but to go down, the sun
without hint of its will to disobey, hung
for the moment suspended from the rapidly
vanishing blue of the sky, like a pearl
from a pole, a streetlamp, or a chandelier
which, with the emptying of the ballroom,
stops swinging of a sudden and is so still
it seems it never could have moved. Still,

The sun was going to go down, but first
invited my rowboat to join it, and so I
devised a journey into the eye, and embarked
on it, gliding without work of oars or arms
over the clear and calm watery floor, cool
as an ice-skating rink, peaceful as sleep,
summery as myself in a boy's blue overalls,
freedom's uniform, fishing at memory's end.

Blind Hopes

The camera gave the moment a posthumous shock.

—*Walter Benjamin*

Everyone is hungry, no one is safe,
Too few faces, too many facts. And as if
One were following you invisibly,
Ever since childhood, vanishing with you
Down subway steps, briefcase in hand, still
It takes the eyes by surprise, some getting
Used to: a loud smile, a posthumous
Shock, as the gap left by the crowd
Of hurrying others dominates the scene,
Like a line which suddenly decides

301

To move by itself, with neither finish
Nor start in sight, a blur or a smear
Exploding in the silence of an ear
Too small for the shell in which
The power of the sea used to be
Contained, once upon a time, and nothing else.

PAMELA ALEXANDER

interface

They watch each other.
One knows how to read and drive
the car. The other
sees colors, strokes the cat.

One dislikes darkness
because he wants to see things coming.
The other enjoys it; it makes him
anything. He is
a sitting bush. A planet.

They hold a shape up
to daylight. One sees a square,
the other a triangle.
They don't argue about it:
each knows he is right.

One plays with matches, wanting
to make a small day. The other
uses headlights. He wants to
get somewhere, find the end
of a straight line.
He wants to fill the square
with cheering people.

Where the road ends, they hear
ducks squabbling on the river.
They walk along the bank, wary.
From the other side
a single person looks back:
themselves.
The world is a square
and a triangle. They stay

inside the shapes.

Flight

for Amelia Earhart

A series of white squares, each
an hour's flying time, each with instructions
in pencil: the organized adventure. "Carelessness
offends the spirit of Ulysses." She suspends herself,
as he did, in the elements, finds
reason turns to motion, caution to design.
"One ocean led naturally to
another." The earth led naturally to the sky
after a look at a thing of wood and wire
at the state fair in Des Moines, after the sting
of snow blown from the skis of training planes
near Philadelphia.
                              The rumble of the red and gold
Electra wakes the air, shakes stars
down their strings until
they hang outside the cockpit, close enough
to touch. The squares, short days,
take turns showing her senses
what to do. The fragrance of blooming
orange orchards carries to considerable
altitudes. "No one has seen a tree
who has not seen it from the air, with
its shadow." Lake Chad is huge, shallow,
brightened by the wings of cranes and maribou
storks. The Red Sea is blue; the White and Blue Niles,
green; the Amazon delta a party of currents,
brown and yellow, distinct. Beyond

the clutter of sensations, the shriek and clatter
of tools at landing fields, she prepares
herself, like the engine, for
one thing. Flight
above the wine-dark shining flood

is order, makes the squares
come and go, makes the plane
a tiny gear that turns the world. "Of all those things
external to the task at hand, we clutch
what we can."
                    She leaves the plane briefly to join
a crowd of Javanese walking up a beautiful mountain.
They laugh and talk, they carry baskets
and various loads on poles. "Sometime
I hope to stay somewhere as long as I like." For

the last long passage she abandons personal items,
souvenirs; also the parachute, useless over the Pacific.
The plane staggers with the weight of fuel.
The squares arrive,
live in her,
subside. The plane
is lighter, then
light. The last square has
an island in it, but does not
show her where.

    Air

It holds us, gently,
together.
It presses out, against the eardrum.
It presses in. It curls
in the palms of our hands

but holds nothing
to itself. It steps over
the sock flung onto the chair, the blouse
on the floor. When we touch in it,
it moves aside—a modest medium

that solid things displace.
The children running down the street

punch through it, leaving
a cut-out shape of each position
floating behind them
for an instant.

It is made of round
spinning things, but
it will adjust to a rectangular space such as
a room.
It's the only company
the old man who stays in his underwear all day
has.
He comes onto the porch at noon
to get more.

People identify it by objects it surrounds.
It is then called "atmosphere."
What people see is
themselves: they approve or they don't,
they leave for good or they come back.
Air is innocent of such judgments, having
no personality to protect.

It has only
a simple habit:
it fills anything.
It occupies entire hotels
in the off season.

It is drawn to emptiness as to
a question it answers. Only a person
can puzzle it: the vacancy interior,
locked behind the eyes.

It stays whole, flows around
the wall, the knife.
We can change it
as much as ourselves, or another person:
very little.

AMANDA POWELL

Leaving Home

The pillows swell with confession;
fine dust piles under the unmade beds.
Nothing is old here, now.
My hands are made of a membrane like shells:
I walk through rooms as if
I had just put something down.
A sharp rain raises mist on the snow outside.
We start late, the morning already over,
my packing thrown in
in a hurry. I am the one who will not be back tonight.
My tongue shapes around cold air
and will not answer.
In the house I am leaving, each person
is becoming a strange, bright light.

My ice man begins to move.

In my arms sometimes I dream he's a woman
when his voice rises from a warm root;
then he can try anything.
He is sturdy as his upbringing
He's educated. I listen:
through his chest I hear a garden.
I found him after a storm, shining,
compacted: often I walked around him.
In sun the ice man's edges glow;
he leans like a bright tree, beckoning.
All winter, back to back, we dream
of a long rain.

WILLIAM LOGAN

My Father

My father is with some other
Woman. She is not like my mother.

The motel room is dark, but light
Leaks in, and gathers at their right

In pockets by the door and shades.
She teaches in the lower grades

Nearby. He says, "I love you,"
In her ear. It is not true.

He rubs her leg again, but soon
Looks at his watch. Still afternoon,

The children with their books walk
Home from school. One throws a rock

Against a passing car, which slows,
But then speeds on. Ironing clothes

At home, my mother waits for winter,
Or cries, or thinks of dinner.

The Goose Fish

They say the Sirens called a man
With his heartbeat, put to song.
Now the night sings, rain beats the flats.
The lathery tide withdraws. Before the rain,
Walking the flats, I found a fish,

Dead at the last low tide,
A goose fish, each jellied eye transfixed
By the clouded sky, like two moons
Hung in the night's opposite quarters.

The dead season storms into being,
Dredging fragments, detritus, to spread
With an even hand along the shore.
We find broken boxes, clay pipes, pottery
From unknown sailors or wrecks, lured
To their individual ends.
                    The tide falls away
And returns, its only ancestor itself. But the fish
Survives from some more difficult time,
Each sailor had a father, I have a father still
To call me home to a winter burial.
The dead do not awaken, their progeny
Devour them, their memories, reach
The full flood of their own maturity,
And fall back. They fall back.

THOMAS LUX

There Are Many Things
That Please Me

The loam and lungs of dreams
to begin with. Certainly
those sailboats drifting across
your thighs please me. I'm pleased
with the courage of the surgeon
who performs open heart surgery
on a mosquito and I'm so pleased
I can hardly describe the mosquito's
courage. I'm pleased
that ice is finally beginning to lose.
I'm pleased, very pleased
with the lizards and fish
and whoever else taught us
this language. Nothing pleases me more
than not having my tongue drawn back
in terror. I'm even pleased
with my strength: I can lift
these gray aspirin to my lips,
I can tear this match from a matchbook.
I'm pleased we can say to our children:
It's almost time to sing! All
these things please me, so many
things please me. I'm pleased
in the evening when I lower
the shade and what looks like the last
snowflake in the world doesn't
float by. But most of all
I'm pleased with myself, pleased
with myself in the same way
I'd be pleased with a man
who carries a sack
of disdain, a somewhat silver
disdain, nevertheless, a disdain,—

and who is beginning to spill it,
spill it the same way the sun
climbs a hill early in the morning:
gradually, with a determined heat, leaf
by leaf and branch over branch.

Green Prose

I'm writing this with green ink so you'll believe me
when I tell you I'm a nature poet. I'm a nature poet.
You know, the ones close to the earth—the green
water, blood, and breath of it all. . . Don't move!:
there's a grasshopper on my shoulder and I think he's
about to nuzzle my ear!—Surely you're getting tired
of this nature bunk by now. Nature is bunk! In the
dry cave of every nature poet's mind there is a desire
to torture chipmunks, those most detestable of small
rodents, to stomp Lady Slippers, etc. And who hasn't
dreamed of strangling a deer with his bare hands, of
tearing out the liver and devouring it? Let's get this
straight once and for all: green is the symbol of
death and mourning, it's the official color of lamen-
tation. Everyone but me has lied to you: *there is no
green*—unless it comes from gashes, from far inside
the blackest lung, *no green,* don't think about it or
you'll die.

Poem to My Creditors
(—after Alan Dugan)

You'll never get me Banks, Hospitals,
Real Estate Agencies, Collection Agencies,
National Brotherhood of X-Ray Technicians,
never. . . You make me nervous, though, all silent
now for a few months—as if you were ganging

up on this guy Lux, forging your little blades
into one big blade: O I'm *nervous!* I should
warn you, Pals: forget it. You won't get it,
a drop, of my green blood. I have none.
I have none therefore I cannot owe none.
Besides, you'll never find me: everywhere
you look I'm gone. None and gone. None and gone—
they barely half-rhyme
like my wallet, bank account, and credit.

ANN DEAGON

The Death of Phidias

Between the trial for embezzlement and the trial for impiety
Phidias sickened in prison and then went mad.
When we brought his water he flung it on the floor
and scraped up the hard-packed clay with his rotting nails
to mold crazed figurines:
a man with his head attached between his legs
and on his shoulders a great erection,
women with holes in their breasts and teats
         on their buttocks,
babies with too many arms and not enough legs,
a hunched hermaphrodite with a giant hand
coming out of its rump like a rooster's tail.

When they put him on trial he crowed like a rooster himself
and when they asked what he meant by that he said
he was Zeus the Cock crowing so the sun would rise.
They convicted him, but some of the jurymen wept
and all of them shuddered. Back in prison
while his friends were scraping up his fine
he ate the crusts of his bread but molded the insides
with his saliva into indefinable forms
intestines that flowered into cabbages,
livers with claws, things without names or existence
except in his hands and our half-tainted eyes.

He began to save his excrement in a corner
saying that it was his earnings to pay his fine.
That last day when we found him he had torn
one wrist with his toenail, blending the oozing blood
into the lumpy mass. It lay beside him,
his masterpiece self-portrait, like him dead,
only a little more stinking than his flesh
and not much difference for long between them.

313

We buried it beside him, never spoke of it.
We jailers learn too much we don't dare tell.
Some nights I dream that the whole acropolis
quakes into chaos and the long walls crumble
golden Athena melts and this bright air
glooms into prison dimness and the stench
of Athens rotting.

The Owl Pellet

At tree level owl and professor blink
yellow noon, doze in the musty
hollow of tree and office, ruffle
dreaming of things furry astir by dark.
Below on Founders' steps two boys
dissect the pellet from the owl's late hunt,
catalogue the indigestible
debris of bone, claw, fur, one perfect skull
its jaw askew, recognizably rat.

Young friends, you are on the track: classify,
enumerate, set down in your tablets
THE OWL HAS MADE A POEM, THE GRAY PROFESSOR
HAS VOMITED HER HUNT. I will analyze
my latest for you: this image, students,
is carved from Gloria Spoletti's thighbone
unforgettable for twenty years;
here just the profile of a blind black boy
seen from a passing streetcar, there the hump
of my old crippled fencingmaster, rotten
with all unanswered letters. When the greedy
guzzle of living sates us and the bones
stick in our craw—we cough up a poem.
It clears our throat if not our consciences.

So go, boys, and do you likewise.
Learn the wisdom of the owl professor:
FLY OPEN-GULLET INTO THE DARK,
BOLT DOWN WHATEVER SCURRIES.
Noontime's time enough to cull
the skeleton from the feast.

Jigsaw Puzzle

"Ici commence li livres du graunt Caam"
Marco departs from Venice on my table:
that gush of merchantry and years
splattered to fragments like all history,
the painter's seeing sawn to crazy shapes,
a therapy of touch and color. Piece
by piece St. Mark's lofts up the gilded four
horses, the doge's palace furbishes
its colonnades, below in the piazzetta
a butcher hawks magenta carcases
(so interlock church, state, and our deep-dyed
carnality), and undergirding all
like grace, the Adriatic's blue pervasion.
Marco takes ship with blessings and rich freight;
across the foreground's brief foreshortened sea
lions couch in the heraldic wild.

Traveler, the world you pieced together
from far-flung segments of your life, now curls
at edges: carmine, saffron, verdigris
brown into speculation. All our launchings
confirm that the Grand Khan is dead. Design
lingers only in shapes, in colors, touch
and turning. Year by year we reconstruct
these tedious puzzles, these tedious poems.

Going Under

I

Ellen enters the pool:
eleven, breastless she breasts the water
her sutured heart powerful as surf
(below her nipple the red cicatrice
remembers intensive care).

Splashes close her eyes, she shouts
    Marco. . .
the writhing children plunge,
scatter, their round mouths answer
    Polo. . . Polo. . .
She launches blind
through the liquid sounds
catching at her childhood.

II

Face down on this glass-bottomed bed I map
sunken Venice, luminous through
layered aquamarine. The girl
Elena enters the church of San Marco:
maidens swirl about her, pearls
entwine her emerald hair.
Inside the nave phosphorescent as
a sea-cave candles waver, the round
notes of choirboys surface like bubbles.
Nicolo Polo takes his bride.
She will name their son Marco.

III

And was he like a god
who entered you, got you with child,
cast off for Constantinople, visited
the court of the Grand Khan, and like
Odysseus lingered twenty years?
Penelope had choices. Yours dissolved
in that first rending childbirth when
the flesh canal ran water, blood, and your
fresh life into the brackish grave.
Venice, where every burial is
a putting to sea.

IV

Face up in the embrace of stone you age.
Brine condenses on your lashes like
crystalline coronals, your eyes awash
inside the liquefying skull; your skin
paler than beauty wrinkles in the saline
secrecy of the vault.

                      Marco full grown
greets his father at the wharf. Of all
his merchantry the fairest bargain this,
and most Venetian: a woman for a son.
Not the doge only
marries the sea.

V

Ellen, Elena, sisters, we are wed
to an interior and bloody sea.
We take its tides to realms exotic as
Marco's extravagances, hazard there
our damask bodies.

Ellen, daughter,
the scalpel has made you perfect, arch your
perfect body downward, plunge past
heraldic Venice wreathed in tentacles,
sea-caves and mermen, past the glimmering past,
lower than color, luminescence, tide—
where in dark-standing deep
egg-laden hulks
celebrate their soundless nuptials.

KRAFT ROMPF

Finger Spelling

Let's say it's not language
the deaf transmit,
but something graceful against the retina,

a clarinet
played without the need for music
inside the eye.

Badly out of tune like an old piano
I move towards you
in our house full of windows.

On your face a hidden message,
secretly your fingers draw me to it.

The Distant Lover

Run the razor along your lip.

The wind hauls its cargo of snow
over the roofs.
A wolf
slumps in a hammock of red snow.

O when we bleed
we swoop like airplanes from our lives.

A Song for Solomon Heine

The women whisk their skirts to the fiddle
turning in a glass room.
Here in the hallway
the moon melts to wax on the floor.

*

He threw her to a pit of fire flies.
She swhirled through night and forest.

*

O Solomon,
come dance on the mountain,
sing with me; let me touch your smooth white hair.

O Solomon,
tie my love to a window.

Islands for Seurat

1

Last night she danced with her lover
on the river of lights.
Now she fishes with another,
baiting her hook with a dot.

2

He has travelled by coach to ask for her hand.
She must refuse.
Just yesterday Papa remarked how this young man's dots
looked more like yellow bees
than orchids.

3

The children are unsure of their parents.
It is Sunday. Everyone is all dressed up
in colored dots.

4

The dog is smiling.
Several dots smell like cheese.

NAOMI LAZARD

In Answer to Your Query

We are sorry to inform you:
The item you ordered
is no longer being produced.
It has not gone out of style
nor have people lost interest in it.
In fact, it has become
one of our most desired products.
Its popularity is still increasing.
Orders for it come in
at an ever growing rate.
However, a top-level decision
has caused this product
to be discontinued forever.

Instead of the item you ordered
we are sending you something else.
It is not the same thing,
nor is it a reasonable facsimile.
It is what we have in stock,
the very best we can offer.

If you are not happy
with this substitution
let us know as soon as possible.
                As you can imagine
we already have an accumulation
of letters such as the one
you may or may not write.
To be totally fair
we respond to these complaints
as they come in.
Yours will be filed accordingly,
answered in its turn.

Ordinance on Failure

Now that you have lost
there is no going back to start again
no matter how much you would like to.
We do not operate a time machine,
cannot take on the repair
of what has already happened.
It is official. You have failed.
Everyone knows about it or soon will.
We could say
this is an extraordinary situation
for you, but we cannot.
Unfortunately
it is all too ordinary.
Come to terms, as best you can,
with the facts. After what
you have been through
don't despise yourself now
any more than is necessary.
Nobody knows better than we do
how you have struggled
for a bit of the precipice.
Sympathy is in order;
there is nothing we can do.
You are a failure. There it is.
We continue to try our utmost
to find a solution to this problem.
The best minds at our disposal
are working in closed session.
You can imagine the difficulties.
Each failure is unique;
sui generis is the term for it.
Reflect on this.
The comfort you find in its truth
will sustain you.

The Last Covenant

for the wolves

The sun marks the sea with a sign,
last bright sickle of light.
We drive the wind before us
into the darkness, quickly
across the domain of waters, fast

as your fur and my hair can fly.
What a bird would say I feel
on my lips; the words breaking out
in pairs, two by two as those other
animals went from the flood.

Moonlight flickers and melts
on the air; one final leap
into the deep night and we hit
land. Now we're creeping like sap
from a tree while the ground is wet

underfoot, and the beetle's sound
is a gong. On our knees in the end,
back to the roots of the heart.
This is the place, the wind
made flesh; the greens and all

movement are one. We can just see
the brilliant faces of cubs
looking out. All night I must kneel
at the gates of the house without
doors. Morning comes like a knife

between my eyes. I must roll back
my tongue and forget my own
language of lies. Then my body
remembers, my feet grow as sure
as your own of those deepest

retreats where we all sleep
together. The ways of the trees
open for me, defying the guns,
the numbers of enemies
who are stalking the woods

where we live now as we should live,
our bodies close as the ringing
of bells. I am one with you at last,
a guardian of paradise,
with a helmet of fiery leaves

and nothing more. I know we will not
survive. I see us already ablaze,
trapped in a circling fire.
The killers stand on its edge,
triggers cocked, quick on the draw

and ready. We have only this
moment. You push your face
into my hand; I hold you hard
at my side, bless you again.
A cry holds us both in its arms.

Ordinance on Winning

Congratulations.
The suspense is over. You are the winner.
The doubts you have had
concerning the rules of the contest,
about the ability and fairness of the judges,
were ill-founded. The rumors
pertaining to a "fix"
have been exposed as nonsense.
The contest is fair and always has been.
Now that the results are in

your prize will be sent to you
under separate cover. Be sure you have
your social security number
or other proper identification
for the postman.
Upon receiving it
contact us immediately in order that you
may be notified of further developments,
ensuing publicity,
other honors which will be forthcoming.
If by some chance your prize does not arrive
as scheduled, do not bother to inform us.

Our responsibility is discharged
with this announcement.
In the event that you do not receive
your prize, there is no authority
to whom you can turn
for information or redress.
We advise you to wait patiently
for your prize
which will either come or not.

ARTHUR SMITH

The Killing

Tonight I walk straight into it
into the field, into the bleak
stump carcassed meadow burning moonlight
as my feet burn against these oats, chokecherries
and the lightning splintered chaparral.

When you get too close the poison oak turns red.
I am too close.

The deer sees
nothing but my lone light:
The moon's come down to gather him
into my numb right cheek.

One light,
my shoulder pelted by the rip
explosion in my hands, on my hands
the smell of pepper, and the deer
sees nothing
but the light that's been
locked into his eyes. His eyes

empty blue. I knew
I'd have to punch a knife into his neck
to bleed him while his nose
foams into the oats,

as the sideways waltz
of ticks begins, the choked
ticks drowning in their cut loose food,

the meadow frosted moonlight
setting in my mouth, my slick hands

and his dry eyes, his hollow blue
I throw my hands and face into.

LINDA GREGG

Figures Near a Bridge

Everything formal.
The man turns around
and makes a sound.
It is a long cry.
The woman turns around
so you can see her face.
The look on her face
is the sound he made.

For My Friend Michele (1966-1972)

So the subject is death again today. How easy that poem is.
How easy and how good all my poems on death have been.
Instant Praxitelian. Instant seventy-five year old photograph
of my grandmother when she was a young woman
                                        with shadows
I imagine were blue around her eyes. The beauty of it.
Such guarded sweetness. What a greed of bruised gardenias.
Oh Christ, whose name rips silk, I have seen raw cypresses
so dark the mind comes to them without color.
Dark on the Greek hillside. Dark, volcanic, dry and stone.
Where the oldest women of the world are standing
                                        dressed in black
up in the branches of fig trees in the gorge
knocking with as much quickness as their weakness will allow.
Weakness which my heart must not confuse with tenderness.
And on the other side of the island a woman
walks up the path with a burden of leaves on her head,
guiding the goats with sounds she makes up,
and then makes up again. The other darkness is too easy:
the men in the dreams who come in together to kill me with knives.
There are so many traps, and many look courageous.

The body goes into such raptures of obedience.
But the huge stones on the desert resemble
nobody's mother. I remember the snake.
After its skin had been cut away, and it was dropped,
it started to move across the clearing.
Making its beautiful waving motion.
It was all meat and bone. Pretty soon it was
                              covered with dust.
It seemed to know exactly where it wanted to go.
Toward any dark trees.

The Men Like Salmon

The heart does not want to go up.
The bones whip it there, driving it
with terrible music of the spirit.
The flesh falls off like language,
bruised and sick. Sick with the bones.
Rotten with sorrow. Leaving everything
good or loved behind. The bones
want to go. To end like Christ.
Ah, the poor flesh. The mute sound
of flesh against stone. Emptied
of maidens and summer and all
the fine wantonness of life.
The bones insist on immaculate changes.
Io carrying bees close to her heart.

The Apparent

When I say transparency, I don't mean seeing through.
I mean the way a symbol is made when an X is drawn over (
As the world moves when it is named. In the sense
of truth by consciousness, which we translate as *opposites.*

The space we breathe is also called distance.
Presence gives. Absence allows and calls,
until Presence holds the invisible, weeping.
Transparent in the way the heart sees old leaves.
As we become more like the hills by feeling.
I mean permanence. As when the deer and I
regard each other. Ah, there was no fear then.
When she went with her young from the meadow
back into the nearly night of the woods,
it was because the rain came down suddenly harder.

Andromache Afterwards

She has only the memory and is cut loose
from legality. She listens to a calling
which is only in a place like heaven.
Andromache weeps in the new castle
and no one can turn her from it.
She demands to be taken to the sea.
Will not stop weeping until then.
There are things on the earth shared by the gods, she says.
Kee Kee are the birds in the air of both.
Shoosh is the sea sound reaching Thessaly,
and there is no way to get that weeping
out of your mind.
She remembers a high hurrying overhead.
She tells us (in the sewing room,
motionless in front of the loom) she hears
skirts dragging against stone and the sound
of metal. The sound of bodies and pleading.
Otherwise, she does nothing but study Greek.
She becomes more distant and unafraid every day.
She weeps, but seems happy.
And will not cease demanding we escort her to the sea.

Not Singing

When you stop looking at the garden,
the eye begins furtively to acknowledge the barren poplars
and the giant spruce and the firs.
And so it is with this maid in me not asking to be saved.
Another one takes her place. Neither merciful
                                    nor unmerciful.
There are almost no flowers to be looked at anyhow.
No flowers to bear having an opinion about.
And the more it rains the less flowers there are.
The flowers, they say, all along were the journey.
Like the branches thrown down before the little
                                    donkey feet
of Christ on the way to glory.
I would not have it different.
Ruin is everywhere. The plague of soft rain endless.
We sing of loss because the only voice they gave us
was song and reasoning. It is not love we are after.
Not love. Not singing. But a somber thing.
A going to the opening and entering.

THE ARDIS ANTHOLOGY OF NEW AMERICAN POETRY

Photographs and Biographical Notes

NUMERICAL KEY TO PHOTOGRAPHS
(Photographers in parentheses)

1. Tess Gallagher
2. Daniella Gioseffi (Fox)
3. Michael Berryhill (Stephen Anton Gillies, IMAGE)
4. Gerard Malanga (Aram Saroyan)
5. Doug Flaherty
6. David Lehman
7. Marisha Chamberlain
8. R.T. Smith
9. Richard Williams
10. Thomas Lux (Jean Kilbourne)
11. Dale Matthews
12. Amanda Powell
13. Judith Moffett (Elinor J. George)
14. Lynn Strongin (Christa Fleischman)
15. Gary Soto
16. T.J. Porter (Bruce Dart)
17. Billy Collins (Art Plotnik)
18. Brian Swann (Linda Scheer)
19. Jane Katz (Isabelle Goodman)
20. Keith Althaus (Larry Maglott)
21. Emery E. George
22. William Logan
23. Ryah Tumarkin Goodman
24. Yvonne
25. Martin Steingesser
26. T.R. Jahns
27. Bart Schneider
28. Rodger Kamenetz
29. Heather McHugh
30. Pamela Alexander (Kenneth Alden)
31. Lemuel Johnson
32. Jordan Smith (Doris Low)
33. William Heath
34. Kraft Rompf (Jan Starr)
35. Margaret Gibson (Richard Morgan)
36. Robert Hahn (Sarah Gleason)
37. Mark Axelrod
38. Katha Pollitt
39. D.C. Berry
40. Thom Swiss
41. Arthur Smith
42. Tom O'Grady
43. Jonathan Sisson (Judy Olausen)
44. Ronald Wallace
45. Carol Frost (Richard Frost)
46. Ron Bayes (Tony Ridings)
47. Gary Miranda
48. Ann Deagon
49. Charles O. Hartman
50. Neil Baldwin
51. Michael Waters
52. John Skoyles (Linda Fry)
53. David Perkins (Gary Bodenhausen)
54. Ellen Bryant Voigt (B.J. Sheedy)
55. Alan Ziegler (Harry Miller)
56. Susan Snively
57. Ahmos Zu-Bolton (E. Thompson)
58. Ronald Wallace
59. Tom House
60. Harry Stessel
61. Larry Zirlin (Harry Greenberg)
62. Dennis Trudell
63. Michael Hogan
64. Naomi Lazard
65. Peter Meinke
66. Susan Hartman
67. Kirtland Snyder
68. Terrance Keenan
69. Rachel Hadas
70. Hunter Brown
71. Arthur Smith (Ronnie Smith)
72. Ronald Koertge
73. Henry Petroski
74. Philip Dacey
75. Binnie Klein
76. Ed Ochester
77. Virginia R. Terris (Don Wolf)
78. Sharon Leiter
79. Charles Cantrell
80. David Kirby
81. Marie Harris
82. Lynn Sukenick (Michael Harris)
83. Laurance Wieder (Gini Alhadeff)
84. Charlotte Alexander
85. Peter Trias
86. David McKain (Howard Park)
87. Rudy Shackelford
88. Patricia Goedicke (Miki Boni)
89. Cleopatra Mathis
90. Steven Orlen
91. Linda Gregg
92. David Childers
93. John Morgan
94. William J. Higginson

2

4

5

6

8

7

9

10

11

12

14

15

16

17

18

19

20

21

24

22

23

25

30

1

32

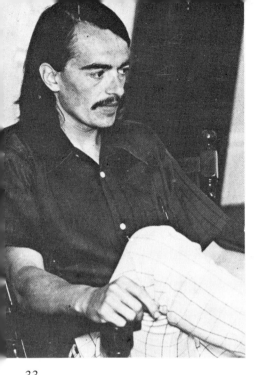

33

34

35

36

37

38

39

40

41

43

42

44

45

47

46

48

49

51

50

52

53

54

55

56

57

58

59

60

61

62

64

63

65

66

67

69

68

70

71

72

73

74

75

76

77

78

79

80

81

82

84

85

83

86

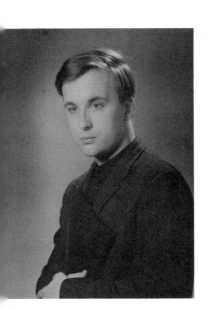

87

89

90

93

91

94

92

THE PURDUE DEPARTMENT
PRESENTS

A Free Public Lect

WILLIAM HIGG
Poet and Transl

HAIKU IN ENGLIS
FROM EZRA POUN
TO THE NEW HAIK
AND BEYOND

ursday, No

St

BIOGRAPHICAL NOTES

CHARLOTTE ALEXANDER—Born Indiana. Published: *Carleton Miscellany, Arts in Society, Poem, Niagara Magazine, Concerning Poetry, Prairie Schooner, Poetlore, Prism International, West Coast Review, The Small Pond*. Lives, teaches (College, CUNY), writes, NYC. Edits literary magazine, *Outerbridge*.

PAMELA ALEXANDER—Grew up in Natick, Mass. Graduated from Bates College and the University of Iowa Writer's Workshop. Her poems have appeared in *The Atlantic Monthly, Field* and *Poetry*. She is currently a Writing Fellow at the Fine Arts Work Center in Provincetown, Mass.

KEITH ALTHAUS—Born 1945 York, Pa. Tried college and dropped out. Joined staff of Fine Arts Work Center in Provincetown in 1973. Published *APR, New Yorker, Iowa Review, Harper's, Greensboro Review, Provincetown Poets, Epoch, Poetry*.

MARK AXELROD—Finishing a Master's degree in Comparative Literature at Indiana University. Work has appeared in *New York Quarterly, West Coast Poetry Review, Assemblings VI, West Conscious Review, De Tafalronde*. 1977 Candidate for a Fulbright Fellowship in Literature.

NEIL BALDWIN—Born in NYC, June 21, 1947. Poems appearing widely in magazines (*American Poetry Review, West Coast Review, Cape Rock, Rapport*, etc); first collection, *Seasons*, from salt works press 1976. Living in Buffalo NY, teaching in Poets in the Schools, editing *The Niagara Magazine*.

RON BAYES—Born in 1932 in Oregon, has lived in Japan and Iceland; since 1968 has made North Carolina home; edits *St. Andrews Review*. Three books in print, most recently *King of August* (Curveship); published in *Prairie Schooner, Tri-Quarterly, West Coast Review, Phoebe* and elsewhere.

BRUCE BENNETT—Born Philadelphia, 1940. Taught at Harvard, Oberlin, Wellesley; currently Director of Creative Writing at Wells College. Co-founded and served as editor of *Field* and *Ploughshares*. Poems have appeared in *The Nation, Counter/Measures, Ploughshares, Identity*, elsewhere.

D.C. BERRY—33, born in Vicksburg, MS, and currently teaching at The U. of S. Miss. Center for Writers, has published 200 poems and one volume.

MICHAEL BERRYHILL—Born 1945, raised in Houston, Texas. PhD., University of Minnesota, American Studies. Currently teaching at Vassar College. Poems have appeared in *American Preview, Inscape, Penny Dreadful*. Working on a collection of poems tentatively titled *First Light*.

HUNTER BROWN–Born June 8, 1954, Cincinnati, Ohio. Educated in Cincinnati and attended Hamilton College. Winner of Academy Poetry Prize, 1976.

MICHAEL BURKARD–Grew up in Rome, NY, attended Hobart & Smith College and the Univ. of Iowa Writer's Workshop. Two collections of poems appearing in 1977: *In a White Light* (L'Epervier Press), and *The House (a series)* (Sheol Press).

CHARLES CANTRELL–Born in Jacksonville, Fla. Feb. 4, 1945. Works have appeared in many little magazines, including *Abraxas, The Chowder Review*, and the anthology: *For Neruda, For Chile*. At present studying poetry and fiction-writing in Goddard College's new MFA Program.

MARISHA CHAMBERLAIN–Born in 1952 in Sarasota, Florida. Poems have appeared in *Dacotah Territory, Rapport, Sojourner*, and elsewhere. Currently St. Paul's community poet, and co-director of Minnesota Poetry Out Loud. Received NEA Fellowship for writers, 1976.

DAVID CHILDERS–Born and raised in Mt. Holly, NC, started writing poems at 15. Published in *Carolina Quarterly, St. Andrews Review, Cold Mountain Review, Pequod, Rolling Stone* and many others. Now selling classified ads.

BILLY COLLINS–Born 22 March 1941, NYC. PhD., UC-Riverside. Assistant Professor of English, Lehman College (CUNY). Editor of *The Midatlantic Review*. Poems have appeared in an exultation of magazines. Currently working on a biography of Keith Richards.

PHILIP DACEY–Born, 1939, St. Louis. Awards: Discovery '74, NEA and Woodrow Wilson Fellowships, Borestone and Yankee First Prizes. Poems in *Esquire, Paris Review, Nation, American Review, Poetry*, others. Coordinator of Creative Writing, Southwest State University (Minnesota). First book, *How I Escaped from the Labyrinth and Other Poems* (Carnegie-Mellon University Press) due in Spring 1977.

ANN DEAGON–Born 1930 in Birmingham, teaches Classics at Guilford College. Publications include: *Poetics South* (Blair, 1974); *Carbon 14* (U. Mass., 1974); *Indian Summer* (Unicorn, 1975); *Women and Children First* (Iron Mountain, 1976); forthcoming *There Is No Balm in Birmingham* (Godine, 1977).

DOUG FLAHERTY–Born in Lowell, Mass., April 1939. Published in *New Yorker, The Nation, The North American Review, Poetry Northwest*, and others. Currently teaching at the Univ. of Wisconsin at Oshkosh.

PETER FRANK–born 1950 in NYC. Writes on art for *ArtNews, Art in America*, and other critical journals. Poetry published in *Roy Rogers, The World, First Issue, Just Before Sailing, Sun*, and *The Coldspring Journal*.

CAROL FROST–Born in Mass. in 1948. Poems have appeared in *Antaeus, Poetry Northwest, Prairie Schooner, Shenandoah*, etc. A chapbook,

The Salt Lesson (Graywolf Press), appeared in 1976. Writing fellowship at Syracuse University, a Breadloaf Scholarship, and a new manuscript, *Common Places*.

TESS GALLAGHER—Born northwest Washington. Two books: *Stepping Outside* (Penumbra Press, 1974) and *Instructions to the Double* (Graywolf Press, 1976). NEA grant, CAPS award, Elliston Award for the Best Book of Poetry published by a small non-profit press in US, 1976. Now living in Clinton, NY.

EMERY GEORGE—Teaches at Univ. of Michigan, is founding editor of *Michigan Germanic Studies*. His two collections of verse are *Mountainwild* and *Black Jesus* (both Kylix, 1974. Currently translating poetry by Miklós Radnóti.

MARGARET GIBSON—Born February 17, 1944, in Philadelphia, Pa. Lives and writes in New London, Connecticut, and teaches in English Dept. at Connecticut College. Recent chapbooks include *Lunes* (Some of Us Press), and *On the Cutting Edge* (Curbstone Press).

DANIELA GIOSEFFI—Widely performs poetry, dance, and music in shamanistic rituals. Published variously in leading anthologies and periodicals. Teaches creative writing for Poets-in-the-Schools. Awarded two grants from NY State Council on the Arts. A novel from Doubleday, 1977. Born 1941, Orange, NJ.

PATRICIA GOEDICKE—Born in Boston, June 2, 1931; brought up in New Hampshire by my parents, Helen Mulvey and John McKenna, M.D. First book: *Between Oceans* (Harcourt, Brace); second is *For the Four Corners* (Ithaca House).

RYAH TUMARKIN GOODMAN—Born in Russia, came to America at age six. Poems have appeared in *The Atlantic, Saturday Review, The Nation, The Horn Book, Epoch, Epos, Etc: A Review of General Semantics, Chicago Tribune, Forum, Imprints Quarterly, Osiris, Granite, Zahir, Voices, Voices International, Patterns, Green River Review,* and others.

LINDA GREGG—Has published in *The American Review, Antaeus, The Paris Review, The New Yorker,* and *The American Poetry Anthology* (Avon). She lives in Marin County, California.

RACHEL HADAS—Born NYC, 1948, educated Radcliffe. Has lived in NY, Vermont, Greece. Teaching Fellow and student in poetry for 1976-7 in Writing Seminars, Johns Hopkins Univ., Baltimore. Book *Starting from Troy* (Godine, 1975); poems in *Poetry, Harpers,* etc. etc.

ROBERT HAHN—Has published two books of poetry, *Routine Risks* (Abattoir Editions) and *Crimes* (Lynx House Press). Teaches at Simon's Rock and lives in Great Barrington, Mass.

MARIE HARRIS—Born Nov. 7, 1943, NYC. Work has appeared in *Poetry NOW, Mountain Moving Day* (anthology), and others. Book, *Raw*

Honey (ALICEJAMESBOOKS, Cambridge, MA 02138).

CHARLES O. HARTMAN–Born August 1, 1949, Iowa City. Harvard A.B., Washington University M.A., PhD.–dissertation on free verse. Poems in *Poetry, Poetry Northwest, Descant.* Teaching poetry at Northwestern. Forthcoming book, *Making a Place* (Godine, 1978).

SUSAN HARTMAN–Born June 1, 1952 in NYC. Work has appeared in *Carolina Quarterly, City, Hanging Loose, Kansas Quarterly, Poem* and *Forum.* Now teaching in the New York State Poets-in-the-Schools program.

WILLIAM HEATH–Born Youngstown, Ohio, June 27, 1942. Poems published in *Approaches, Bitterroot, Green River Review, Midatlantic Review,* others. Currently assistant professor of English at Vassar College.

WILLIAM J. HIGGINSON–Born NYC 1938, has poems, prose, translations in *Madrona, Center, Whole Word Catalogue 2, Small Press Review, Haiku Anthology,* edits *Haiku Magazine,* lives in Paterson, works in NJ PITS.

MICHAEL HOGAN–Born July 14, 1943, Newport, R.I. Work has appeared in *Kayak, The American Poetry Review, The Greenfield Review* and others. Currently co-editing and translating an anthology of contemporary Mexican poetry.

TOM HOUSE–Born 1949. Attended Univ. of N. Carolina. Poems published in *Nausea, Willmore City, Barbeque City, Modularist Review,* and others. Currently residing among friends in Nashville, Tn.

T.R. JAHNS–Born April 5, 1949, Hobbs, N.M. Graduate of Creative Writing program, Univ. of Arizona. Published in *Poet and Critic, Hiram Poetry Review, College English, The Smith,* and others.

LEMUEL JOHNSON–Born of Sierra Leone parents in Northern Nigeria. Stories in *The Literary Review, Journal of New African Literature and the Arts, African Writing Today.* Poems collected in *Highlife for Caliban* (Ardis, 1973). Teaches in English Dept. at Univ. of Michigan.

LORING JOHNSON–Born East Texas, 1951, currently working offshore for an oil company. Owner of Isa Pragbhara Press.

RODGER KAMENETZ–Born 1950, Baltimore. Poems in *Southern Poetry Review, Carolina Quarterly, Yale Literary Magazine, Gulfstream, St. Andrew's Review.* Pamphlet, *The Stationhouse* (Laughing Man, 1973). Teaches: Maryland Poet in Schools, Community College of Baltimore.

JANE KATZ–Grew up in Hartsdale, southern New York. Graduated from Kirkland College in creative writing. Winner of Watrous prize, 1973.

TERRANCE KEENAN–Born Munich, 1947. Lived variously in Europe, USA, Africa, and the Carribean. Presently owner and sole operator of a small bookstore in Clinton, NY. Married to someone quite remarkable.

ROLLY KENT–Work in *The Atlantic Monthly,* and others. Chapbook *The*

Wreck in Post Office Canyon (Maguey, 1976). Lives in Tucson.

DAVID KIRBY—Born Baton Rouge, Louisiana, 1944. PhD. Johns Hopkins. Now teaching at Florida State Univ. Latest book is *The Opera Lover*, a chapbook of poetry.

PETER KLAPPERT—Born Rockville Centre, NY, Nov. 14, 1942. Collections: *Lugging Vegetables to Nantucket* (Yale Univ., 1971); *Circular Stairs, Distress in the Mirrors* (Griffin, 1975) and *Non Sequitur O'Connor* (Bits, 1977). Currently writer-in-residence at William and Mary.

BINNIE KLEIN—Born 26 years ago, Newark, NJ. Published in *Minnesota Review, Panache, New, The Drummer, Goddard Journal, Center*, others. Honorable Mention 1975 Mademoiselle College Poetry Competition; First Prize, 1975 Chase Going Woodhouse Poetry Prize.

RONALD KOERTGE—Born April 22, 1940. Poems in *Wormwood Review, Poetry Now, Beloit Poetry Journal*, others. Books: *Meat* and *The Hired Nose*, both from Mag Press. *The Father Poems*, Sumac Press. Others. Now teaching at Pasadena City College.

HERBERT KROHN—Vietnam veteran and physician. Poetry in *The New Yorker, The Nation*, and others. Now living in Cambridge, Mass.

NAOMI LAZARD—Born Philadelphia, published in *New Yorker, American Review, Ohio Review, Paris Review*. First book, *Cry of the Peacocks*, published by Hiram Haydn, with Harcourt Brace. Forthcoming book, *Ordinances* (Ardis).

DAVID LEHMAN—Born NYC 1948. Published in *Poetry, Paris Review, TLS*. Book: *Some Nerve* (Columbia Review Press, 1973). Assistant Professor of English, Hamilton College. Ingram Merrill Foundation Grant, 1976-7.

SHARON LEITER—Born Brooklyn, NY, 1942. Poems and translations have appeared in *RLT, Triquarterly, Ararat, Bitterroot, Cardinal Poetry Quarterly, Cloud Marauder, Pyramid*, others. Currently teaching Russian at Univ. of Virginia.

WILLIAM LOGAN—Born 1950 Boston, Mass. M.F.A. Univ. of Iowa 1975. Poems have appeared in *New Yorker, Poetry, American Review*, others.

THOMAS LUX—Born Dec. 1946, Mass. Books: *Memory's Handgrenade* and *The Glassblower's Breath*. NEA grant 1976. Currently teaching at Sarah Lawrence College.

CYNTHIA MACDONALD—Former opera-singer, now lives between NYC and Baltimore, where she teaches at Johns Hopkins. Has published two books, both Braziller, *Amputations* (1972) and *Transplants* (1975).

HEATHER McHUGH—Born '48 California. Lowered '49-'65 Virginia. Colleged '65-'69 Mass. Made livings in British Columbia, Colorado, Missouri, NY state. Teaching at SUNY Binghamton. Poems since '68 in *New*

Yorker, Harpers, Antioch Review, others. Book: *Dangers* (Houghton-Miflin, 1977).

DAVID McKAIN—Born Punxsutawney, Penn. Book: *In Touch* (Ardis, 1975). Presently working on a series of poems on the life and times of Marcus Aurelius, Roman archetype for much that's uniquely American: drugs, imperialism, meditation.

GERARD MALANGA—Born 1943, NYC. Author of 21 books and chapbooks to date, most recent being *Rosebud* (Penmaen Press) and *Ten Years After: The Selected Benedetta Poems* (Black Sparrow Press).

CLEOPATRA MATHIS—Born August 16, 1947, Ruston, Louisiana. Work is forthcoming in *American Poetry Review* and other magazines. Presently completing an M.F.A. in writing at Columbia Univ.

DALE MATTHEWS—Born Feb. 25, 1949, Sanford, NC. Poems have appeared in *Intro 3, The Hollins Critic, Hyperion, The Southern Poetry Review,* others. Presently teaching in Maryland Poets-in-the-Schools Program.

PETER MEINKE—Born Brooklyn 1932, now Director of Writing Workshop at Eckerd College, St. Petersburg, Fla. Latest publication: *Lines From Neuchatel* (Konglomerati Press, 1974); recent winner of PSA Gustav Davidson award. Forthcoming book: *The Night Train and the Golden Bird* (Pitt Poetry Series, 1977).

GARY MIRANDA—Born Bremerton, Washington, 1938. Work published in *Transatlantic Review, London Magazine, Chelsea, Mademoiselle,* and elsewhere. *Story* Creative Awards: second prize, 1969; first prize, 1970. Poetry Society of America and Christopher Morley Awards in 1973.

JUDITH MOFFETT—Born Louisville, 1942, raised in Cincinnati. First book of poems is *Keeping Time* (LSU, 1976); has also published reviews, translations from Swedish, and criticism.

JOHN MORGAN—Born 1943 NYC, currently living in Fairbanks, Alaska. Work published in *Poetry, New American Review, Chelsea,* etc., and the anthology, *The Young American Poets.*

ED OCHESTER—Born Brooklyn, NY, 1939. Teaching at Univ. of Pittsburgh. *Dancing on the Edges of Knives* (U. of Missouri Press, 1973) and four small press chapbooks. Poems most recently in *APR, Paris Review, Poetry Now, Liberation,* etc.

TOM O'GRADY—Born Baltimore, 1943. Latest work in *New Letters, Epoch, Contemporary Literary Scene.* Co-founder and Editor of *The Hampden-Sydney Poetry Review.* College teacher, winegrower in Virginia.

PERRY OLDHAM—Born 1943. Degrees from Oklahoma State University, University of Maryland, University of Oklahoma. Air Force: 1966-70. Presently teaching school. Poems in several magazines and anthologies.

A collection of war poems, *Vinh Long*, published by Northwoods Press.

STEVEN ORLEN–Born Holyoke, Mass. 1942. One chapbook, *Sleeping on Doors* (Penumbra Press, 1975), another, *Separate Creatures*, forthcoming from Ironwood Press. Currently teaching at Univ. of Arizona and living in the Elysian Grove Market in Tucson.

DAVID PERKINS–Lives in Kansas City Mo., edits *Chouteau Review*. Poems in *Kansas Quarterly, Prairie Schooner, Dacotah Territory, Big Moon, Harrison Street Review, Stump*; also, writing in *Poet & Critic, National Catholic Reporter*, and others. NEA Fellowship 1973-74.

HENRY PETROSKI–Born NYC 1942. Poems in *Poetry, The Beloit Poetry Journal, Descant, Shenandoah, Prairie Schooner*, and others. 1976 recipient of Illinois Arts Council Poetry Award.

KATHA POLLITT–Born 1949, grew up in Brooklyn. Most recent award: *Nation*-Discovery award 1975. Poems in *The New Yorker, The Atlantic Monthly, The Nation, Mademoiselle, Poetry, Ploughshares*. Currently proofreading and reviewing for various magazines.

T.E. PORTER–Born 1942, Amelia Island, Florida. First Book: *King's Day*, a novella, 1975. *The Cruel Lover in the Blue Bed*, poetry, due this year, and novel about life on the Gulf of Mexico will appear in 1978. Now living in mountains of Pennsylvania.

AMANDA POWELL–Born in Boston Feb. 15, 1955. Poems in Yale *LIT*, *Womenswords*. Senior at Yale, working on translations and critical studies of Spanish women poets.

KRAFT ROMPF–Born Hamburg, Germany, 1948, came to US 1953. Work in *The Falcon, Poetry Now, The New York Quarterly, Dryad, Gulfstream, Nutmeg*, others. Anthologized in *Starting from Paumanok, Anylion*. Presently teaching at Essex Community College in Baltimore County.

BART SCHNEIDER–Spent the last year out of the country, now lives in San Francisco.

RUDY SHACKELFORD–Musician by profession. Born 1944, Gloucester County, Virginia. Poems in *New Yorker, Sewanee Review, New Republic, Virginia Quarterly Review*, numerous others.

JONATHAN SISSON–Born in Massachussetts in 1941, now living in Minnesota. Poetry available in *Dim Lake,* a three-person anthology published by Red Studio Press.

JOHN SKOYLES–Raised in Jackson Heights, NY. Past Writing Fellow at Fine Arts Work Center in Provincetown. Work in *APR, North American Review* and *Ohio Review*. Recipient of NEA grant for 1976-77. Lives in Dallas, teaches at SMU.

ARTHUR SMITH– Born 1948, Stockton CA. Poems in *Stand, The Ohio*

Review, Chicago Review, Poetry NOW, Rapport, Southern Poetry Review and others. Served as Poet-in-Residence at San Joaquin Delta Coll.

JORDAN SMITH—Born in Upstate NY, attended Hamilton College and Empire State College in Rochester. Recipient of Academy of American Poets Award. Currently living in Upstate NY.

R.T. SMITH—Author of *Waking Under Snow* and founder of *The Cold Mountain Review* in the NC mountains, now teaches at Auburn, suffers from terminal paranomasia, likes large dogs, has an Appalachian State U. M.A.

SUSAN SNIVELY—Born New Orleans, Sept. 6, 1945, grew up in Kentucky. Poems have appeared in *Poetry, The American Scholar, The Massachusetts Review, The Hollow Spring Review.* Lives in Lenox, Mass. and teaches at Smith College.

KIRTLAND SNYDER—Born Bronxville NY, July 3, 1948. Poems in *Foreword, aspen leaves, Poet Lore, The Hartford Courant, Poetry, Prose, Plays: An Anthology.* Currently teaching high school English in West Hartford, Connecticut. Contributor Bread Loaf Writers' Conference 1975.

GARY SOTO—Born 1952. 1975 Discovery-*The Nation* award. First book, *The Elements of San Joaquin*, received the US Award of the International Poetry Forum for 1976 and was published by the Univ. of Pittsburgh.

WILLIAM SPRUNT—Born North Carolina 1921. Poems in *Southern Poetry Review, The Nation, Cold Mountain Review, St. Andrews Review.* Book, *A Sacrifice of Dogs,* to be published.

MARTIN STEINGESSER—Poems and articles in *The New York Times, Evergreen Review, The Village Voice, The American Poetry Review, The Ohio Review.* Teaching in the New York State Poets-in-the-Schools program. Born NYC 1937.

HARRY STESSEL—Born 1939, Dunkirk, NY. Work in *Xanadu, Beloit Poetry Journal, Ascent, Kansas Quarterly, Focus/Midwest, Mississippi Review, Quarry, Hiram Review, Minnesota Review.* Taught at Reed, at Grinnell. Currently on Fulbright in Sweden, 1976-79.

LYNN STRONGIN—Born 1939 NYC. Poetry in *Poetry* (Chicago), *New York Quarterly,* etc. Latest books: *Paschal Poem* (chapbook) (Sunring, 1976); *A Hacksaw Brightness* (chapbook) (Ironwood, 1977); *Toccata of a Disturbed Child* (Fallen Angel, 1977). NEA grant 1972. Lives in N. Mexico.

LYNN SUKENICK—Author of *Houdini* (Capra Press); *Water Astonishing* (Ragnarok); and *Problems and Characteristics* (Avocet). Past recipient of NEA grant, now teaching creative writing and literature at UC-Santa Cruz.

BRIAN SWANN—Born in England in 1940, now Associate Professor of English at The Cooper Union, NYC. Poetry: *Roots; The Whale's Scars.* Prose: *Liking the Sky.* Co-translator of five books of translation.

THOM SWISS–Born Chicago 1952. Work in *Transatlantic Review, Beloit Poetry Journal, Intro 7, Wisconsin Review, Chicago Tribune Magazine, Mississippi Valley Review, John Berryman Studies, Descant*, etc. Academy of American Poets Prize 1973. Living now in Iowa City.

ROSS TALARICO–Born 1945, Rochester, NY. Graduate work Syracuse Univ. Writer-in-Residence Southern Connecticut State College. Books: *Snowfires* (Best Cellar, 1972); *Simple Truths* (North Carolina Review, 1976). Currently Assistant Professor of English at Loyola Univ. in Chicago.

VIRGINIA R. TERRIS–Born Brooklyn, NY, 1917. Poems in *American Poetry Review, New Letters, The Nation, Modern Poetry Studies, Chelsea, Gravida, Poetry Now*, etc. Book: *Tracking* (Univ. of Illinois, 1976). Currently finishing annotated bibliography, *Woman in America* (Gale).

PETER TRIAS–Born 1948. Taught in Poetry-in-the-Schools Program in Chapel Hill, NC. Work in *The New York Times* as well as in various literary magazines. Chapbook: *That House in Venice* (St. Andrews, 1976). Presently residing in Los Angeles.

DENNIS TRUDELL–Born 1938, Buffalo, NY. I have taught "English" in some colleges and universities and in some I haven't. Anthologized in: *New Voices in American Poetry* (Winthrop), *Quickly Aging Here* (Doubleday Anchor). Last chapbooks: *Avenues* (Best Cellar Press), *Eight Pages* (Abraxas).

ELLEN BRYANT VOIGT–Poems have appeared in *The Nation, Sewanee Review, Shenandoah, Southern Review, Southern Poetry Review, Ohio Review, Iowa Review, Salt Creek Reader*, and others. First book: *Claiming Kin* (Wesleyan Univ., 1976). Now teaching at Goddard.

RONALD WALLACE–Born 1945, Ph.D. Univ. of Michigan, 1971. Poems in *The New Yorker, Poetry, Iowa Review*, among others. Currently teaching writing and modern literature at the Univ. of Wisconsin in Madison.

W.S. WARDELL–Born in Detroit in 1948. Left as soon as possible. Currently dividing my residence between New York and Paris, producing and directing tasteless porno movies for which I receive large sums of money. Poetry for the peasants.

MICHAEL WATERS–Born NYC 1949. M.A. SUNY Brockport, M.F.A. Iowa. Book: *Fish Light* (Ithaca House, 1975). Living now in Athens, Ohio.

LAURANCE WIEDER–Latest volume of poetry is *No Harm Done* (Ardis 1975). Currently living in NYC.

RICHARD WILLIAMS–Born October 20, 1944, attended the University of North Carolina, where he received an M.A. in Spanish Literature. Work has appeared in *Lillabulero, The Carolina Quarterly,* and *Ironwood*. A book, *Savarin*, will be published by Ardis in 1977.

YVONNE–Born Pennsylvania 1948. Work in *New York Quarterly, Best*

Friends, Aphra, Ms., Shantih, Sunbury, etc. Recipient NEA and Mary Roberts Rinehart Fellowships. Currently poetry editor at *Ms.*

ALAN ZIEGLER—Born August 21, 1947, Brooklyn, NY; published in *Paris Review, American Poetry Review, Poetry Now, The Village Voice*, etc.; Co-editor *Some* and Release Press; conducts poetry workshops for, among others, Teachers and Writers Collaborative.

LARRY ZIRLIN—Born 3/29/51, Newark, NJ. Books: *Hedged Bets* (Release Press, 1973) & *Sleep* (Wyrd Press, 1976). Work in *Village Voice, Abraxas, Paris Review,* others. Currently an unemployed printer free-lancing layout & design jobs.

AHMOS ZU-BOLTON II—Born Poplarville Miss. 1948. Work in: *Yardbird Reader, Black World, Painted Bride Quarterly, Essence, Washington Review of the Arts*, etc. Authored: *A Niggered Amen* (Solo Press, 1975). Publisher of Energy BlackSouth Press in Washington D.C.